First Workshop on Ancient Language Translation (ALT 2023)

Macau, China
5 September 2023

Editors:

Bin Li
Shai Gordin

ISBN: 978-1-7138-9036-2

Printed from e-media with permission by:

Curran Associates, Inc.
57 Morehouse Lane
Red Hook, NY 12571

Some format issues inherent in the e-media version may also appear in this print version.

Association for Computational Linguistics
209 N. Eighth Street
Stroudsburg, Pennsylvania 18360

Phone: 1-570-476-8006
Fax: 1-570-476-0860

acl@aclweb.org

Additional copies of this publication are available from:

Curran Associates, Inc.
57 Morehouse Lane
Red Hook, NY 12571 USA
Phone: 845-758-0400
Fax: 845-758-2633
Email: curran@proceedings.com
Web: www.proceedings.com

ALT2023

MTS Machine Translation Summit 2023

September 4-8, 2023 Macau SAR, China

Proceedings of ALT2023:
First Workshop on Ancient Language Translation

September 5, 2023

Editors: Bin Li, Shai Gordin

Preface

The proceedings include the papers accepted for presentation at the First Workshop on Ancient Language Translation (Machine Translation from Ancient Languages to Modern Languages, ALT2023 for short)[1]. The workshop was held on September 5th in Macau SAR, China, co-located with the 19th Machine Translation Summit (MT Summit 2023)[2].

The workshop seeks to provide an opportunity to learn about the challenges and latest developments in the field of machine translation for ancient languages. Participants engaged in discussions and hands-on activities to develop a deeper understanding of the field and the techniques used to address the unique challenges posed by translating texts written in ancient languages. The workshop concluded with a discussion of the results of the hands-on activities and a summary of the key takeaways from the workshop. Participants left the workshop with a deeper understanding of the field of ancient language machine translation and the tools and techniques used to address its unique challenges. In this year's workshop, we proposed shared tasks on Machine Translation for Ancient Chinese and Cuneiform languages (Akkadian and Sumerian), respectively, to provide an opportunity to address the unique challenges faced by ancient language machine translation. The topics of the workshop were closely related to the special features of translation in ancient languages that distinguish them from modern languages and have a significant impact on machine translation.

ALT 2023 is the venue for the second edition of EvaHan, an event dedicated to the evaluation of NLP tools for Ancient Chinese. EvaHan [3] is a series of international evaluations focusing on the information processing of Ancient Chinese. In 2022, together with EvaLatin for automatic analysis and evaluation of Ancient Latin, EvaHan 2022 focused on the task of Part-of-Speech tagging. More than ten teams participated in the evaluation, and Evahan2022 achieved the best results ever in the field.

EvaHan2023 focused on Machine Translation from Ancient Chinese to Modern Chinese/English. EvaHan2023 was organized by the Center of Language Big Data and Computational Humanities at Nanjing Normal University, College of Information Management at Nanjing Agricultural University, School of Economics & Management at Nanjing University of Science and Technology.

Training data for evaluation was excerpted from the Twenty-Four Histories (dynastic histories from remote antiquity till the Ming Dynasty), the Pre-Qin classics and ZiZhi TongJian (资治通鉴), Comprehensive Mirror in Aid of Governance). The test data was only provided in Ancient Chinese, which was derived from the ancient Chinese books Jinlouzi (金楼子) and Houshan Tanshong (后山谈丛). The test dataset consisted of about 2,000 sentences. Each participant could submit runs following two modalities. In the closed modality, the resources each team could use are limited. Each team could only use the training data, and the pre-trained models supplied by the organizers. In the open modality, however, there was no limit on the resources, data and models. Participants were required to submit a technical report for the task in which they participated. EvaHan received a total of eight technical reports, all of which were briefly reviewed by the organizers to check for correct formatting, accuracy of reported results and rankings, and overall presentation. There is also an overview paper in the proceedings detailing some specific aspects of the second EvaHan, such as the datasets, metrics, and results of the shared task.

Besides EvaHan, ALT 2023 hosted also the first edition of EvaCun[4], an evaluation series of NLP tools for the Ancient languages written in the Cuneiform script (3,400 BCE-75CE), organized by Adam Anderson (Data Science Discovery Partner, UC Berkeley, California), Shai Gordin (Digital Pasts Lab,

[1] https://github.com/GoThereGit/ALT
[2] https://mtsummit2023.scimeeting.cn/en/web/index/
[3] https://github.com/GoThereGit/EvaHan
[4] https://digitalpasts.github.io/EvaCUN/

Ariel University, Israel), and their research students. Cuneiform is one of the earliest writing systems in recorded human history (ca. 3,400 BCE-75 CE). Hundreds of thousands of such texts were found over the last two centuries in the Middle East. Most of these texts are found on a clay or stone medium, and are written in Sumerian and Akkadian, beside relatively smaller corpora (still in the tens of thousands) in Elamite, Eblaite, Hittite, Hurrian, Urartian, Hattian, and Luwian, as well as languages which use alphabetic Cuneiform like Ugaritic and Old Persian. EvaCun 2023 consists of three machine translation tasks – Akkadian (in Cuneiform) to English, Akkadian (transcription) to English and Sumerian (transcription) to English, based on the corpora of royal, administrative, and financial texts we provide. For the Akkadian part we used the corpora from the Open Richly Annotated Cuneiform Corpus (ORACC)[5]. Chronologically, the great majority of the texts are Neo-Assyrian (NA) and the best attested genres are the royal inscriptions (2,997) and administrative letters (2,003). Nevertheless, the chosen corpus represents a variety of genres. For the transcription to English we used 56,160 sentences, where we treat each sentence as an independent example for training. We call them in these guidelines "sentences", even if they are made up of a single word, a group of words, a phrase or a group of phrases. This is mostly because Cuneiform does not have punctuations that separate sentences like modern languages do. For the Sumerian part we used a corpus from the Cuneiform Digital Library Initiative (CDLI) and of a neural network-based encode-decoder architecture for English-Sumerian and Sumerian-English. The Sumerian data is only available in transliterated form. The project carries out English to Sumerian and Sumerian to English Translation using a parallel corpus of about 20K sentences for both languages as the parallel corpora. We evaluated the performance of the cuneiform/transcription/Sumerian-to-English machine translation model based on BLEU. EvaCun received one technical report overdue. The task will move to the next year.

[5]http://oracc.museum.upenn.edu/

Organizers:

Shai Gordin (shaigo@ariel.ac.il), Ariel University, Israel
Bin Li (lib@njnu.edu.cn), Nanjing Normal University, China

Program Committee:

Adam Anderson, US Berkeley (USA)
Congjun Long, Chinese Academy of Social Sciences (China)
Dongbo Wang, Nanjing Agricultural University (China)
Ethan Fetaya, Bar-Ilan University (Israel)
Gabriel Stanovsky, Hebrew University of Jerusalem (Israel)
Konstantin Margulyan, Ariel University (Israel)
Liu Liu, Nanjing Agricultural University (China)
Luis Sáenz, Ariel University/Heidelberg University (Israel/Germany)
Minxuan Feng, Nanjing Normal University, (China)
Morris Alper, Tel Aviv University (Israel)
Renfen Hu, Beijing Normal University (China)
Sanhong Deng, Nanjing University, (China)
Si Shen, Nanjing University of Science and Technology (China)
Stav Klein, Ariel University (Israel)
Xiaodong Shi, Xiamen University (China)
Yudong Liu, Western Washington University (USA)

EvaCUN 2023 Organizers:

Adam Anderson, University of California, Berkeley (USA)
Shai Gordin, Ariel University (Israel)
Stav Klein, Ariel University (Israel)
Konstantin Margulyan, Ariel University (Israel)

EvaHan 2023 Organizers:

Dongbo Wang, Nanjing Agricultural University (China)
Si Shen, Nanjing University of Science and Technology (China)
Minxuan Feng, Nanjing Normal University (China)
Chao Xu, Nanjing Normal University (China)
Lianzhen Zhao, China Pharmaceutical University (China)
Wenlong Sun, Nanjing Tech University (China)
Kai Meng, Nanjing Agricultural University (China)
Liu Liu, Nanjing Agricultural University (China)
Wenhao Ye, Nanjing Agricultural University (China)
Weiguang Qu, Nanjing Normal University (China)
Bin Li, Nanjing Normal University (China)

Sponsors:

Phoenix Media

Jiangsu Wenku

Table of Contents

Conference Program

Monday, September 5, 2023

14:00–14:10 Opening Remarks

Invited Talks

14:10–14:30 Prof. Zhiwei Feng, Xinjiang University (China)

14:30–15:00 Prof. Jinxing Yu, Peking University (China)

Oral Reports

15:00–15:15 *EvaCun: The first shared task on Cuneiform Machine Translation*
Shai Gordin

15:15–15:30 *EvaHan2023: Overview of the First International Ancient Chinese Translation Bakeoff*
Dongbo Wang, Litao Lin, Zhixiao Zhao, Wenhao Ye, Kai Meng, Wenlong Sun, Lianzhen Zhao, Xue Zhao, Si Shen, Wei Zhang and Bin Li

15:30–16:00 *Coffee Break*

16:00–16:15 *The Ups and Downs of Training RoBERTa-based models on Smaller Datasets for Translation Tasks from Classical Chinese into Modern Standard Mandarin and Modern English*
Stuart Michael McManus, Roslin Liu, Yuji Li, Leo Tam, Stephanie Qiu and Letian Yu

16:15–16:30 *Pre-trained Model In Ancient-Chinese-to-Modern-Chinese Machine Translation*
Jiahui Wang, Xuqin Zhang, Jiahuan Li and Shujian Huang

16:30–16:45 *Some Trials on Ancient Modern Chinese Translation*
Li Lin and Xinyu Hu

16:45–17:00 *Istic Neural Machine Translation System for EvaHan 2023*
Ningyuan Deng, Shuao Guo and Yanqing He

Monday, September 5, 2023 (continued)

17:00–17:15 *BIT-ACT: An Ancient Chinese Translation System Using Data Augmentation*
Li Zeng, Yanzhi Tian, Yingyu Shan and Yuhang Guo

17:15–17:30 *Technical Report on Ancient Chinese Machine Translation Based on mRASP Model*
Wenjing Liu and Jing Xie

17:30–17:45 *AnchiLm: An Effective Classical-to-Modern Chinese Translation Model Leveraging bpe-drop and SikuRoBERTa*
Jiahui Zhu and Sizhou Chen

17:45–18:00 *Translating Ancient Chinese to Modern Chinese at Scale: A Large Language Model-based Approach*
Jiahuan Cao, Dezhi Peng, Yongxin Shi, Zongyuan Jiang and Lianwen Jin

18:00–18:10 Closing Remarks

EvaHan2023: Overview of the First International Ancient Chinese Translation Bakeoff

Dongbo Wang db.wang@njau.edu.cn
Litao Lin litaolin@njau.edu.cn
Zhixiao Zhao 2022114011@stu.njau.edu.cn
Wenhao Ye yewenhao@njau.edu.cn
College of Information Management, Nanjing Agricultural University, Nanjing, 210031, China
Kai Meng mengkai@njau.edu.cn
School of Marxism, Nanjing Agricultural University, Nanjing, 210095, China
Wenlong Sun 287971655@qq.com
School of Foreign Languages, Nanjing Tech University, Nanjing, 211816, China
Lianzhen Zhao buddy_zlz@163.com
School of Foreign Languages, China Pharmaceutical University, 211198, China
Xue Zhao 741081584@qq.com
College of Information Management, Nanjing Agricultural University, Nanjing, 210031, China
Si Shen shensi@njust.edu.cn
School of Economics & Management, Nanjing University of Science and Technology, 210094, China
Wei Zhang 292204510@qq.com
College of Information Management, Nanjing Agricultural University, Nanjing, 210031, China
Bin Li (Corresponding author: libin.njnu@gmail.com)
School of Chinese Language and Literature, Center of Language Big Data and Computational Humanities, Nanjing Normal University, 210097, China

Abstract

This paper presents the results of the First International Ancient Chinese Transalation Bakeoff (EvaHan), which is a shared task of the Ancient Language Translation Workshop (ALT2023) and a co-located event of the 19th Machine Translation Summit 2023 (MTS 2023). We described the motivation for having an international shared contest, as well as the datasets and modalities. The contest consists of two modalities, closed and open. In the closed modality, the participants are only allowed to use the training data, and the participating teams achieved the highest BLEU scores of 27.33 and 1.11 in the tasks of translating ancient Chinese to Modern Chinese and translating Ancient Chinese to English, respectively. In the open mode, contestants can use any available data and models. The participating teams achieved the highest BLEU scores of 29.68 and 6.55 in the Ancient Chinese to Modern Chinese and Ancient Chinese to English tasks, respectively.

Proceedings of ALT2023: First Workshop on Ancient Language Translation, pages 1–14
September 5, 2023, Macau SAR, China.

1. Introduction

As an important carrier of Chinese traditional culture, Ancient Chinese classics is of great value in historical and literary study. Through the translation of Ancient Chinese classics, excellent traditional Chinese culture can be passed on to contemporary readers and the international community, promoting cross-cultural communication and understanding. However, the fact that the morphology, syntax and lexical meaning of Ancient Chinese are quite different from those of Modern Chinese makes it difficult for Modern Chinese translation technology to achieve better results in Ancient Chinese translation.

Machine translation is mainly divided into methods based on statistics and rules, among which methods based on statistics are the main ones. At present, machine translation research mainly focuses on the interlingual translation of modern languages, while there are few studies on the translation of ancient languages. The translation of Ancient Chinese into Modern Chinese is a special kind of intralingual translation, and there are few related studies at present. The lack of parallel corpora between ancient and Modern Chinese is a key factor restricting the research of Ancient Chinese machine translation (Han et al., 2015). The advancement of neural network models such as Transformer (Vaswani et al., 2017) and BERT(Devlin et al., 2019) has spawned a batch of pre-trained language models for Ancient Chinese. Combined with prompt learning technology (Liu et al., 2021), the successful practice of GPT-like large-scale language models has brought new development opportunities for machine translation research in low-resource languages such as Ancient Chinese (Liu et al., 2023).

In the past period of time, there have been many machine translation evaluation competitions for different languages or domainized texts, such as WMT'22 Shared Task on Large-Scale Machine Translation Evaluation for African Languages (Srivastava & Singh, 2022). Many inspiring results have emerged, including machine translation models (Adelani et al., 2022; Kocmi et al., 2022) and translation effect evaluation methods (Freitag et al., 2022). However, there is still a lack of machine translation evaluation competitions for Ancient Chinese. In this context, we held the second EvaHan event (EvaHan2023): The International Ancient Chinese Transalation bakeoff[1]. EvaHan is a series of international evaluation focusing on the information processing of Ancient Chinese (Li et al. 2022). EvaHan2023 is a shared task of the Ancient Language Translation Workshop (ALT2023), which will be held as a co-located event of the 19th Machine Translation Summit 2023 (MTS 2023) in Macao SAR, China.

EvaHan

2023 is the second campaign devoted to the evaluation of Natural Language Processing (NLP) systems for Ancient Chinese with the following aims:

- To investigate the applicability of current MT techniques in Ancient Chinese translation.
- To examine the significant challenges in Ancient Chinese translation (e.g. word order and syntax errors).
- Provide a platform for the enthusiasts of machine translation in Ancient Chinese
- To facilitate machine translation research for Ancient Chinese and the exploration of forefront machine translation technology.

[1] https://github.com/GoThereGit/EvaHan

2. Task

EvaHan2023 consists of two translation tasks: Ancient Chinese to Modern Chinese (a2m) and Ancient Chinese to English (a2e).

- Ancient Chinese to Modern Chinese machine translation is the process of translating Ancient Chinese sentence in traditional Chinese characters to Modern Chinese in traditional Chinese characters or simplified Chinese characters.
- Ancient Chinese to English machine translation is the process of translating Ancient Chinese sentence in traditional Chinese characters to English.

All tasks require the original sentences to be automatically converted into target language sentences without human assistance. EvaHan2023 allows the teams to submit translation results in one or two of the above two target languages at the same time. Since Hong Kong, Macao and Taiwan regions of China use Modern Chinese writing characters in traditional form, while mainland of China uses simplified format, in the ancient-to-modern translation task, the participating teams are allowed to submit results in either traditional or simplified format. In the stage of translation quality evaluation, EvaHan2023 uses the text in the same language as the submitted results as a reference. Table 1 shows the forms of original sentences and three kinds of target language sentences.

Tasks	Source Language Sentences	Target Language Sentences
a2m (traditional format)	殘諂之吏，張設機網，並驅爭先，若赴仇敵。	殘暴諂媚的的執法官吏，張開羅網，設立陷阱，並駕齊驅，爭先恐後，好似追趕仇敵一樣。
a2m (simplified format)	殘諂之吏，張設機網，並驅爭先，若赴仇敵。	残暴谄媚的的执法官吏，张开罗网，设立陷阱，并驾齐驱，争先恐后，好似追赶仇敌一样。
a2e	殘諂之吏，張設機網，並驅爭先，若赴仇敵。	Cruel and slanderous officials have spread broad nets for me, and they encourage one another against us. It is as if they pursued an enemy.

Table 1: Examples of Modern Chinese Translation and English Translation

3. Dataset

The datasets of EvaHan2023 consists of two parts: training dataset and test dataset. The training dataset, with both Ancient Chinese source text and corresponding Modern Chinese reference translation and English reference translation, is provided for participating teams to train and validate their machine translation models. The test dataset is used to scoring and ranking the machine translation models performance of the participating teams, consisting of Ancient Chinese source text provided to participating teams and corresponding Modern Chinese reference translation and English reference translation remained by conference affairs before the submission deadline.

3.1. Data Format

All evaluation data are .txt files in Unicode (UTF-8) format, arranged by two fields of source language and target language to form a sentence level parallel corpus, as shown in Table 2 and Table 3.

Table 2 shows examples of the Ancient Chinese to Modern Chinese parallel corpus. The left column is the Ancient Chinese text, while the right column is the corresponding Modern Chinese (traditional Chinese format) texts.

Ancient Chinese	Modern Chinese (Traditional Chinese format)
后妃表	后妃表
后妃之制，厥有等威，其来尚矣。	后妃的制度，有它的等级威儀，它的由來很久遠。
元初，因其國俗，不娶庶姓，非此族也，不居嫡選。	元朝初年，因襲蒙古的習俗，不娶異姓，不是后族的，不處在可以選爲正妻的地位。
當時使臣為舅甥之貴，蓋有周姬、齊姜之遺意，歷世守之，因可嘉也。	當時的史臣以爲皇族后族的尊貴，原有周姬、齊姜的遺意，歷代都遵守它，本來是可以表彰的。

Table 2 : Examples of the Ancient Chinese to Modern Chinese (Traditional Chinese format) corpus

Table 3 shows examples of the Ancient Chinese to English parallel corpus. Sentences on the left side is in Ancient Chinese, and on the right side is in corresponding English.

Ancient Chinese	English
杜密素與李膺名行相次，	Du Mi had shared in reputation with Li Ying,
起，對之揖，勸令從學。	He stood up and bowed to him, then urged him to study.
濟陰黃允，以俊才知名。	Huang Yun of Jiyin was known for his outstanding talents.
兵士喜悅，大小皆出。	Officers and men were delighted, and they all went out to take part.

Table 3 : Examples of the Ancient Chinese to English corpus

3.2. Training data

Training data is excerpted from the *Twenty-Four Histories*(dynastic histories from remote antiquity till the Ming Dynasty), the Pre-Qin classics and *ZiZhi TongJian* (资治通鉴, Comprehensive Mirror in Aid of Governance). The *Twenty-Four Histories* is the general name of the twenty-four official histories of various dynasties in ancient China; the Pre-Qin classics are the historical materials of the Pre-Qin period (Paleolithic Period ~ 221 B.C.), which have an important position in ancient books, including history books and sub-books; *ZiZhi TongJian* is a chronological history book compiled by historians of the Northern Song Dynasty, covering sixteen dynasties from 403 B.C. to 959 A.D. over a span of 1362 years. The ancient Chinese classic texts in the corpus feature both diachronicity (i.e. spanning thousands of years) and synchronicity (i.e. covering the four traditional types of Chinese canonical texts *Jing* (经), *Shi* (史), *Zi* (子) and *Ji* (集)).

Descriptions about the overall parallel texts for machine translation are presented in Table 4.

Parallel Data	Source Data scale	Target Data scale
Ancient Chinese to Modern Chinese parallel texts of *Twenty-four Histories*	9,583,749 characters	12,763,534 characters

Ancient Chinese to English parallel texts of Pre-Qin canonical texts and *Zizhi Tongjian*	618,083 characters	838,321 words

Table 4 : Details of training data in EvaHan2023

3.3. Test Data

The test dataset for evaluation consists of 2,071 Ancient Chinese sentences with the corresponding translations in Modern Chinese and English. The Ancient Chinese sentences in test data is excerpted from the *HouShan TanCong(后山谈丛)* and *Jin Lou Zi(金楼子)*. The Modern Chinese and English translations of *HouShan TanCong* are firstly translated through Baidu's classical Chinese translation function, and then proofreaded and perfected by Chinese classical literature experts and English experts. *Jin Lou Zi*'s Modern Chinese translation comes from *Jin Lou Zi*'s translation and commentaries. The English translation was initially obtained through Baidu's classical Chinese translation function, and then proofread and perfected by three English experts.

4. Evaluation

4.1. Scoring Metrics

EvaHan2023 applies BLEU and CHRF to evaluate the quality of submitted translations.

BLEU: BLEU (Bilingual Evaluation Understudy) (Papineni et al., 2002) is an indic ator for automatically evaluating the quality of machine translation. By comparing the machine translation results with the reference translation, the degree of n-gram overlap and the number of matches are calculated to obtain the quality score of the machine translation. Generally, a higher BLEU score indicates that the machine translation result is closer to the reference translation.

Although BLEU has been widely used to evaluate the quality of machine translation, different studies have different optional parameter settings for BLEU (Post, 2018). SacreBLEU(Post, 2018) aims to solve the above problems. It is a toolkit for machine translation quality assessment, developed by Facebook AI Research, which provides a set of parameter setting schemes for standard data sets, and stipulates different language texts and word segmentation algorithm. In order to evaluate the translation quality of each model more reasonably, this study uses SacreBLEU as a specific evaluation tool, setting tokenizer to 'char', and the rest of the parameters remain at default values. EvaHan applies the offical SacreBLEU project (Post, 2017/2023) to do the evaluation.

CHRF: CHRF(Character n-gram F-score) (Popović, 2015), an indicator for evaluating the quality of machine translation systems, is mainly used to evaluate the similarity between machine translation output and reference translation.

The biggest difference beteen BLEU and CHRF is that CHRF evaluates the translation quality in units of words, while BLEU is a word-level translation quality evaluation method. Compared with BLEU, CHRF has the following advantages: First, it can better capture phenomena such as phrase matching and word reordering; second, it can better evaluate the performance of machine translation models in lower-resource language pair translation tasks; in addition, CHRF can also balance precision and recall by using different n-gram sizes. In this study, the word-level n-gram size of CHRF is set to 6, and the smoothing function is selected as "exponential decay". EvaHan applies the offical CHRF code (*ChrF - a Hugging Face Space by Evaluate-Metric*, n.d.) to do the evaluation.

4.2. Two Modalities

Each participant can submit runs following two modalities. In the closed modality, the resources each team could use are limited. Each team can only use the training data and the following pre-trained models listed in Table 5. Other resources are not allowed in the closed modality.

Pre-Trained Model	Language	Description
SikuRoBERTa[2]	Ancient Chinese	Ancient Chinese RoBERTa pre-trained on high-quality *Siku Quanshu*(四库全书) full-text corpus.
Chinese-RoBERTa-wwm-ext[3]	Modern Chinese	Modern Chinese pre-trained RoBERTa with Whole Word Masking strategy.
RoBERTa[4]	English	Pre-trained model on English with MLM objective.

Table 5 : Pre-trained models for closed modality

In the open modality, however, there is no limit on the resources, data and models. Annotated external data, such as the components, Pinyin of the Chinese characters, word embeddings, dictionaries, knowledge graphs, etc. can be employed. But each team has to state all the resources, data and models they use in each system in the final report and manual corrections for translaton results are not allowed.

4.3. Procedures

The open registration period for the competition is from February 15th to March 25th, 2023. The training data set will be available for download on April 1, 2023 and test dataset released on June 7, 2023. Deadlines for submission of translation results and technical reports are June 22 and June 31, 2023, respectively. The evaluation results of each team were returned on June 23, 2023. The deadline for submitting the Camera Ready version of technical reports is July 15, 2023. EvaHan2023 is held at the ALT2023 workshop co-located with the MTS2023 conference in Macao on September 5th, 2023.

5. Participants and Results

5.1. Participants

Table 6 gives the basic information of the participating teams and their submitted results. A total of 9 teams took part in EvaHan2023, submitting 18 translation results. Among them, 8 teams are from colleges and universities, and one is an individual team. All teams submitted translation results in Modern Chinese, two of which submitted translation results in Simplified Chinese. There are four teams that submitted English translation results.

Team \ Task			a2m (traditional)		a2m (simplified)		a2e	
ID	Name	Affiliation	C	O	C	O	C	O
1	BIT	Beijing Institute of Technology	1	0	0	0	1	0

[2] https://huggingface.co/SIKU-BERT/sikuroberta
[3] https://huggingface.co/hfl/chinese-roberta-wwm-ext
[4] https://huggingface.co/roberta-large

2	CUHK	The Chinese University of Hong Kong	1	0	0	0	1	0
3	ISTIC	Institute of Scientific and Technical Information of China	0	1	0	0	0	1
4	L&C	Individual	1	0	0	0	0	0
5	NJU	Nanjing University	1	0	0	0	0	0
6	NJUCM	Nanjing University of Chinese Medicine	0	1	0	1	0	1
7	PKU	Peking University	2	2	0	0	0	0
8	SCUT	South China University of Technology	0	0	0	2	0	0
9	USST	University of Shanghai for Science and Technology	1	0	0	0	0	0
Total Files		18	7	4	0	3	2	2

Table 6 : Result submission status of participating teams in closed (C) and open (O) modalities

5.2. Results

EvaHan2023 uses the BLEU score as the ranking basis, and lists the CHRF score as a reference for readers. Both BLEU and CHRF are calculated in units of corpus, instead of calculating the scores of each single sentence and then averaging them. Among the 18 submitted results, some teams achieved excellent translation results. This paper presents the results of the contest according to different tracks and modalities.

Table 7 and Table 8 show the results of each team in the translation task from Ancient Chinese to Modern Chinese (traditional form). In the closed mode, CHUK scored the best, with a BLEU score of 26.76. In the open mode, ISTIC has the best score, with a BLEU score of 24.34, which is only about 0.17 points ahead of PKU.

Team	BLEU	CHRF
CUHK_1	26.7634	24.5946
PKU_2	24.1719	22.0529
PKU_1	24.1629	22.0451
NJUNLP_1	22.0524	20.5356
BIT_1	21.9485	20.5911
USST_1	21.7537	20.1962
Lemontree_1	20.7738	19.6607

Table 7: The performance of each team in the translation from Ancient Chinese to Modern Chinese (traditional Chinese format) in the closed modality

Team	BLEU	CHRF
ISTIC_2	24.3419	21.4651

PKU_2	24.1719	22.0529
PKU_1	24.1629	22.0451
NJUCM_2	7.3135	10.0544

Table 8 : The performance of each team in the translation from Ancient Chinese to Modern Chinese (traditional Chinese format) in the open modality

In the open modality, two teams submitted three translation results of Modern Chinese in simplified format. We evaluated the translation results of the three submitted Simplified Modern Chinese translations using the Simplified Modern Chinese format test dataset reference translations. At the same time, we also converted other Modern Chinese translation results submitted in the form of traditional Chinese in the open modality into simplified format for re-evaluation, and jointly presented them in Table 9. Their simplified Modern Chinese translations converted from the results submitted in traditional Chinese.

It can be seen from Table 9 that SCUT has achieved the best results, and the BLUE score is 29.68. The results of the two simplified Modern Chinese forms submitted by SCUT are better than the simplified results obtained by converting the traditional Chinese results of PKU. In addition, as far as PKU submitted results in traditional Chinese, after converting to simplified Chinese, the evaluation score of the translation results improved.

Team	BLEU	CHRF
SCUT_2	29.6832	26.1363
SCUT_1	29.5355	26.0515
PKU_2*	26.6438	24.0231
PKU_1*	26.5925	23.9902
ISTIC_2*	24.9170	21.9074
NJUCM_1	9.3807	11.1137

Table 9 : The performance of each participating team in the translation from Ancient Chinese to Modern Chinese (simplified format) in the open modality(The translation result of the team marked with * is converted from their submitted traditional format results)

In this competition, no team submitted results of Modern Chinese translation in simplified format in closed modality. In this regard, we converted all the submitted results in the traditional format in the closed mode to the simplified format, and conducted evaluation with reference to the translation in the simplified format, and the results are shown in Table 10. Compared with the evaluation results of Modern Chinese in traditional form, the top three and their rankings have not changed. CUHK still ranks the first, and the rankings of BIT and L&C have risen.

Team	BLEU	CHRF
CUHK_1*	27.3315	25.0665
PKU_2*	26.6438	24.0231
PKU_1	26.5925	23.9902
BIT_1*	24.3132	22.4501
NJUNLP_1*	24.0682	22.1297
Lemontree_1*	22.5412	21.0501
USST_1*	22.2126	20.5707

Table 10 : The performance of each team in the translation from Ancient Chinese to Modern Chinese (simplified Chinese form) in the closed modality (The translation result of the team marked with * is converted from their submitted traditional format results)

Table 11 and Table 12 show the socres of each team in the Ancient Chinese to English translation task. Under the closed modality, a total of two teams submitted two translation results. The BLEU values are 1.11 and 1.08 respectively, and CHUK's score is slightly better. Under the open modality, two teams also submitted two translation results. The BLEU values are 6.55 and 3.00 respectively, and ISTIC has achieved a clear advantage. The results of the teams on the open modality are significantly better than those on the closed modality.

Team	BLEU	CHRF
CUHK	1.1102	24.2297
BIT	1.1084	23.0841

Table 11 : The performance of the participating teams in the translation from Ancient Chinese to English in the closed modality

Team	BLEU	CHRF
ISTIC	6.5493	26.4452
NJUCM	3.0024	22.8333

Table 12 : The performance of each team in the translation from Ancient Chinese to English in the open modality

5.3. Comparison with Baselines and Toplines

In order to more intuitively present the pros and cons of the translation models and translation results, EvaHan set a baseline and a topline as references. EvaHan2023 selects the single-layer Transformer (Vaswani et al., 2017) model as the baseline model. The parameters of the Transformer model are set as follows: The embedding size or dimensionality of the input tokens is 512; The number of attention heads in the multi-head attention mechanism of the Transformer model is 8; The hidden dimension size of the feed-forward neural network (FFN) within the Transformer model is 512; The number of layers in both the encoder and decoder stack of the Transformer model are 3. EvaHan2023 uses the same training corpus specified under the closed modality to train the Transformer translation model for different tasks, and uses its translation results as the baseline reference translation.

As for the topline, EvaHan2023 selects Baidu's classical Chinese translation API as the topline model, and uses BLEU and CHRF to evaluate the traditional, simplified and English translations. For the English translation results, EvaHan2023 also adds the English translation results obtained by Google's general translation function as a topline reference.

The test data of the baseline model and the topline model are the same test data provided to the participating teams.

5.3.1 Translation from Ancient Chinese to Modern Chinese

Table 13 shows the comparison of the best model with the baseline and topline under the open modality and closed modality. In the task of translating Ancient Chinese to traditional form of Modern Chinese, the Transformer-based translation model was trained for 3 rounds using the parallel corpus of *Twenty-Four Histories*, which consists of 300,000 Ancient Chinese and traditional Chinese translation sentence pairs. Comparing with Table 7 and Table 8, it can be found that all submitted traditional Chinese translation results outperformed the baseline model's translation results. In the open modality, only one team scores below baseline, and no participating team exceeds the topline. Under the closed modality, only CUHK scores more than the topline.

Model Type	Model	BLEU	CHRF
Baseline Model	Transformer	8.9554	10.3511
Topline Model	Baidu Classical Chinese Translation	24.9731	23.0771
Best model in open modality	ISTIC_2	24.3419	21.4651
Best model in closed modality	CUHK_1	26.7634	24.5946

Table 13 : Baseline and topline effects from Ancient Chinese to Modern Chinese (traditional form)

Table 14 shows the baseline and topline in the task of translating Ancient Chinese to simplified format of Modern Chinese, as well as the best results under the open and closed modalities. In the task of translating Ancient Chinese to simplified Modern Chinese, the Transformer translation model was trained for 10 rounds based on 5,899 Ancient Chinese original text from pre-Qin classics and *Zizhi Tongjian* and their corresponding simplified Modern Chinese translation sentence. For the Transformer translation model, 5,899 sentence pairs are not enough to achieve sufficient training, so no good translation results have been achieved. Considering the scores of the translated results in simplified format, there are two teams with a total of 4 submissions exceeding the topline under the open modality; and two teams with a total of 3 submissions exceeding the topline under the closed modality.

Model Type	Model	BLEU	CHRF
Baseline Model	Transformer	9.0368	11.2385
Topline Model	Baidu Classical Chinese Translation	25.5667	23.5617
Best model in open modality	SCUT_2	29.6832	26.1363
Best model in closed modality	CUHK_1*	27.3315	25.0665

Table 14 : Baseline and topline effects from Ancient Chinese to Modern Chinese (simplified format) (The translation result of the team marked with * is converted from their submitted traditional format results)

5.3.2. Translation from Ancient Chinese to English

Table 15 shows the best results for the tasks translated from Ancient Chinese to English under open and closed modalities, as well as the results for the baseline model and the topline model. In this task, the training corpus of baseline model Transformer is 5,899 ancient English parallel sentence pairs of pre-Qin classics and *Zizhi Tongjian*. According to the data in Table 11 and Table 12, the best results on either closed or open modalities did not exceed topline, all teams performed better than the baseline under the closed modality, but neither the closed modality nor the open modality had a better performance than topline. On the whole, the effect of Ancient Chinese to English translation is not as good as that of Ancient Chinese translation to Modern Chinese translation.

Model Type	Model	BLEU	CHRF
Baseline Model	Transformer	0.8901	18.2355
Topline Model①	Baidu Classical Chinese Translation	12.3526	34.5937
Topline Model②	Google Translation	10.7757	31.6446
Best model in open modality	ISTIC_2	6.5493	26.4452

Best model in closed modality	CUHK_1	1.1102	24.2297

Table 15 : Baseline and topline effects from Ancient Chinese to English translation

5.4. Models and Methods

ISTIC: ISTIC uses Transformer as the basic structure of the translation model. ISTIC uses a variety of data preprocessing methods to optimize the quality of the training data set, including removing repetitive sentences, converting traditional characters to simplified ones, unifying punctuation marks, filtering sentence length ratios, and encoding Chinese characters in pinyin. In terms of data enhancement, the team first built an initial model using the training corpus provided by EvaHan, and then used the above model to translate Ancient Chinese data collected from the Internet to form a new parallel corpus. The experimental results show that the new parallel corpus obtained by the above method has a positive effect on improving the performance of the translation model.
BIT: BIT uses Transformer as the basic structure of the translation model. BIT performs word segmentation processing on Ancient Chinese and Modern Chinese in the training corpus, thus constructing a machine translation model encoded in word units. In the data preprocessing part, the team discarded sentences that were too long, taking into account the structural character ISTICs of the model used. In terms of data enhancement, the team first trained a translation model from Modern Chinese to Ancient Chinese based on the training data from Ancient Chinese to Modern Chinese provided by EvaHan, and then used the above-mentioned model to translate Modern Chinese to Ancient Chinese in the training set, thus constructing a new The parallel corpus, the experimental results show that the new data set constructed by this method is beneficial to improve the performance of the model. Based on the expanded new data, the team performed a second round of data augmentation, but experiments found that the second round of data augmentation weakened the performance of the model.
CHUK: CHUK uses RoBERTa and SikuRoBERTa as encoders from Ancient Chinese to English and Ancient Chinese to Modern Chinese respectively, and uses Beam Search to decode the encoded results to obtain translation results.
NJUCM: Based on the Mrasp model, this study fine-tunes the parallel corpus of the Twenty-Four Histories and the ancient English parallel corpus of *Zizhi Tongjian*, so as to evaluate the task. As the application of BERT model in the field of machine translation, the mRASP model uses bilingual parallel corpus in multiple languages for combined training, so that the model fully learns the knowledge of single language and translation between languages. The design idea of the model is similar to the model training fine-tuning paradigm in the current era of large models, and its pre-training task is similar to the downstream task, which can give full play to the performance of the model. However, since there is no Ancient Chinese to English parallel corpus in the pre-training corpus of the mRASP model, its effect is poor in the ancient Chines English translation task. Further increasing the scale of the training data may improve this.
PKU: In this study, the data augmentation method of merging adjacent sentences from the same chapter is adopted, so that the model learns richer contextual information during the training process. At the same time, the first six layer parameters of SikuBERT are used as infrastructure for model building. During the training process, the model training is detected in real time through BLEU and ChrF scores, and the model training is stopped in time, which improves the efficiency of model training to a certain extent. Through data enhancement and model fine-tune, this study has achieved better performance in downstream tasks, and at the same time, it also proves that the data augmentation method adopted in this study has certain feasibility and effectiveness.

SCUT: The study applies large-scale language models to ancient Chinese translation tasks, and performs word list expansion, incremental training and large-scale fine-tuning on the basis of the LLaMA model, and uses a larger training data. Finally, the fine-tuned output of the Ziya-13B(Zhang et al., 2023), a variant of the LLaMA (Touvron et al., 2023), was used as the competition result, and the superior effect was achieved.
NJU: This study used all Twenty-Four Histories corpus for training, and the whole workflow was a standard machine translation process, which employed a standard Transformer-based natural machine translation architecture with the pre-trained model, Chinese-RoBERTa-wwm-ext as the encoder and a randomly initialized decoder. In this study, a relatively large corpus and a join dictionary were used, and only one embedding vector was needed for the same word, which achieved good results while improving training efficiency.
USST: The team built a translation model based on the Transformer architecture, used Siku-Roberta to encode the ancient text, and introduced the method of alternate initialization from Deltalm to initialize the decoder parameters. The process also used BPE-drop to enhance the parallel corpus.

Taken together, pre-trained language models such as SikuRoBERTa and RoBERTa are widely used as encoders. There are also teams that do not use the pre-trained language model in the encoding stage, and achieve good results by refining the training data and adding external knowledge such as pinyin, using the improved Transformer model. There is also a team that applies large-scale language models to Ancient Chinese machine translation. By optimizing the vocabulary, improving the random initialization scheme of unregistered words, and then performing domain-based fine-tuning training on large-scale language models through parallel corpora, they successfully constructed a translation model for Ancient Chinese, and achieved excellent results.

In any case, the scale of high-quality parallel corpora is always a key factor affecting the performance of translation models. In this competition, almost all teams enhanced the training data, and because of the lack of parallel corpus from Ancient Chinese to English, most teams did not achieved the desired effect in the translation task from Ancient Chinese to English.

6. The problems of the text era characteristics

In order to explore the influence of text era characteristics on the performance of machine translation, we split the test data into two parts: *Houshan Tancong* and *Jin Lou Zi*, and re-evaluated the traditional Chinese translation results submitted by CHUK. Table 16 shows evaluation results. From the data in Table 16, we can see that CUHK's translation results of *Houshan Tancong* are significantly better than *Jin Lou Zi*'s. *Houshan Tancong* was written in the Song Dynasty, and *Jin Lou Zi* was written in the Southern and Northern Dynasties. The differences of translation effects are likely to be caused by literary styles in different dynasties.

Test data	BLEU	CHRF
Jin Lou Zi	19.9600	19.2349
Houshan Tancong	36.1354	32.1755

Table 16 : CHUK's performance in the Ancient Chinese to Modern Chinese (traditional Chinese format) translation tasks in *Jin Lou Zi* and *Houshan Tancong*

7. Conclusion

EvaHan2023 is the first bakeoff for Ancient Chinese Mechine Translation. The competition provided a large-scale multilingual parallel corpus of Ancient Chinese. The corpus of this competition with great diachronicity covers pre-Qin classics, *Zhizhi Tongjian*, *Twenty-four Histories*, which were written in different periods and recorded the contents of different periods, providing better support for training high-quality Ancient Chinese translation models.

The participating teams have shown their unique advantages. On the task of translating Ancient Chinese to traditional Modern Chinese, CUHK achieved the best results under the closed modality, and ISTIC achieved the best results under the open modality; on the task of translating Ancient Chinese to simplified Modern Chinese, SCUT achieved the best results under the open modality, and CUHK achieved the best results under the closed modality. On the task of translating Ancient Chinese to English, CHUK and ISTIC achieved the best results under the closed modality and the open modality respectively.

In this competition, the deep trainning language model has been widely used, and the machine translation model from Ancient Chinese to English did not achieve desired results. In future work, we will consider constructing a parallel corpus of Ancient Chinese that includes reference translations in more languages, so as to promote the progress of Ancient Chinese machine translation technology and the spread of excellent traditional Chinese culture to the world.

8. Acknowledgements

This research is supported by the National Social Science Foundation of China major project "Research on the Construction and Application of Cross-language Knowledge Base of Ancient Chinese Classics" (project No. 21&ZD331), Key Project of Ancient Books Work (22GJK006) and National Language Commission Project (YB145-41).

9. Bibliographical References

Adelani, D. I., Alam, M. I., Anastasopoulos, A., Bhagia, A., Costajussà, M. R., Dodge, J., Faisal, F., Fedorova, N., Federmann, C., Guzmán, F., Koshelev, S., Maillard, J., Marivate, V., Mbuya, J., Mourachko, A., Saleem, S., Schwenk, H., & Wenzek, G. (2022, December 7-8). Findings of the WMT'22 shared task on large-scale machine translation evaluation for African languages. In Proceedings of the Seventh Conference on Machine Translation (WMT), pp. 773-800.

Li B., Yuan Y., Lu J., Feng M., Xu C., Qu W., Wang D. (2022). The First International Ancient Chinese Word Segmentation and POS Tagging Bakeoff: Overview of the EvaHan 2022 Evaluation Campaign. In Proceedings of the Second Workshop on Language Technologies for Historical and Ancient Languages, pages 135–140, Marseille, France. European Language Resources Association.

Liu, C., Wang, D. B., Zhao, Z. X., Hu, D., Wu M. C., Lin L. T., Shen S., Li B., Liu J. F., Zhang, H., & Zhao, L. Z. (2023). SikuGPT: A generative pre-trained model for intelligent information processing of ancient texts from the perspective of digital humanities (arXiv:2304.07778). https://doi.org/10.48550/arXiv.2304.07778

ChrF - a Hugging Face Space by evaluate-metric. (n.d.). Retrieved June 29, 2023, from https://huggingface.co/spaces/evaluate-metric/chrf

Devlin, J., Chang, M.-W., Lee, K., & Toutanova, K. (2019). BERT: Pre-training of deep bidirectional transformers for language understanding (arXiv:1810.04805). https://doi.org/10.48550/arXiv.1810.04805

Han, F., Yang T. X., & Song J. H.;S (2015). Ancient Chinese MT Based on Sentence-focused Syntax. Journal of Chinese Information Processing, 29 (2), 103-110,117.

Freitag, M., Rei, R., Mathur, N., Lo, C., Stewart, C., Avramidis, E., Kocmi, T., Foster, G., Lavie, A., & Martins, A. F. T. (2022, December 7–8). Results of WMT22 metrics shared task: Stop using BLEU – Neural Metrics Are better and more robust. In Proceedings of the Seventh Conference on Machine Translation (WMT)(pp.46-68).

Kocmi, T., Bawden, R., Bojar, O., Dvorkovich, A., Federmann, C., Fishel, M., Gowda, T., Graham, Y., Grundkiewicz, R., Haddow, B., Knowles, R., Koehn, P., Monz, C., Morishita, M., Nagata, M., Nakazawa, T., Novák, M., Popel, M., Popovic, M., & Shmatova, M. (2022, December 7-8). Findings of the 2022 Conference on Machine Translation (WMT22). In Proceedings of the Seventh Conference on Machine Translation (WMT)(pp. 1–45).

Liu, P., Yuan, W., Fu, J., Jiang, Z., Hayashi, H., & Neubig, G. (2021). Pre-train, prompt, and predict: A systematic survey of prompting methods in natural language processing (arXiv:2107.13586). https://doi.org/10.48550/arXiv.2107.13586

Papineni, K., Roukos, S., Ward, T., & Zhu, W.-J. (2002, July). Bleu: A Method for Automatic Evaluation of Machine Translation. In Proceedings of the 40th Annual Meeting of the Association for Computational Linguistics (pp. 311–318).

Popović, M. (2015, September). chrF: Character n-gram F-score for automatic MT evaluation. In Proceedings of the Tenth Workshop on Statistical Machine Translation(pp.392–395).

Post, M. (2018). A Call for Clarity in Reporting BLEU Scores. In Proceedings of the Third Conference on Machine Translation: Research Papers, 186–191.

Post, M. (2023). SacreBLEU [Python]. https://github.com/mjpost/sacrebleu (Original work published 2017)

Srivastava, V., & Singh, M. (2022, December 7-8). Overview and results of MixMT shared-task at WMT 2022. In Proceedings of the Seventh Conference on Machine Translation (WMT)(pp.806–811).

Touvron, H., Lavril, T., Izacard, G., Martinet, X., Lachaux, M.-A., Lacroix, T., Rozière, B., Goyal, N., Hambro, E., Azhar, F., Rodriguez, A., Joulin, A., Grave, E., & Lample, G. (2023). *LLaMA: Open and Efficient Foundation Language Models* (arXiv:2302.13971). https://doi.org/10.48550/arXiv.2302.13971

Vaswani, A., Shazeer, N., Parmar, N., Uszkoreit, J., Jones, L., Gomez, A. N., Kaiser, Ł., & Polosu-khin, I. (2017). Attention is All you Need. Advances in Neural Information Processing Systems 30. https://papers.nips.cc/paper/2017/hash/3f5ee243547dee91fbd053c1c4a845aa-Abstract.html

Zhang, J. X., Gan, R. Y., Wang, J. J., Zhang, Y. X., Zhang, L., Yang, P., Gao, X. Y., Wu, Z. W., Dong, X. Q., He, J. Q., Zhuo, J. H., Yang, Q., Huang, Y. F., Li, X. Y., Wu, Y. H., Lu, J. Y., Zhu, X. Y., Chen, W. F., Han T., Pan, K. H., et al. (2022). Fengshenbang 1.0: Being the foundation of Chinese cognitive intelligence. (arXiv:2209.02970). https://doi.org/10.48550/arXiv.2209.02970

The Ups and Downs of Training RoBERTa-based models on Smaller Datasets for Translation Tasks from Classical Chinese into Mandarin Chinese and Modern English

Stuart M. McManus smcmanus@cuhk.edu.hk

Leo Tam 1155158173@link.cuhk.edu.hk

Yuji Li 1155157174@link.cuhk.edu.hk

Songyu Liu 1155191559@link.cuhk.edu.hk

Shuyang Qiu 1155157147@link.cuhk.edu.hk

Daniel Ng ngcheuknamdaniel@link.cuhk.edu.hk

Letian Yu Letian.Yu@link.cuhk.edu.hk

Chinese University of Hong Kong Digital History Lab, Chinese University of Hong Kong, Shatin, Hong Kong, China

Abstract

The paper presents an investigation into the effectiveness of pre-trained language models, Siku-RoBERTa and RoBERTa, for Classical Chinese to Mandarin Chinese and Classical Chinese to English translation tasks. The English translation model resulted in unsatisfactory performance due to the small dataset, while the Mandarin Chinese model gave reasonable results.

1. Introduction

Classical Chinese was the written lingua franca of East Asia for millenia. As with other learned languages (e.g. Latin, Greek, Arabic, Persian, etc.), texts were frequently translated into and out of Classical Chinese, thereby allowing the spread of ideas across linguistic and cultural borders, both within and beyond East Asia's fluctuating polities (Hung, 2005). For example, the extensive translation in multiple directions between Classical Chinese, Manchu and Mongolian with frequent trilingual documents in Qing represents veritable Rosetta Stones that contain information both about word equivalence and pronunciation, as it was common to transliterate terms between languages in the diverse empire (Chang, 2021). Outside the nation, the translation also came at the cost of much effort, since learning foreign languages in an age with few bilingual dictionaries, and fewer teachers, was a tall order. Nonetheless, scholars have highlighted the successes of Persian translators during the Ming dynasty, who prioritized consistency and adherence to the source texts' structure, often glossing identical words in the same manner across different texts (Green and Nile, 2019) while translators for Persian in Ming

Proceedings of ALT2023: First Workshop on Ancient Language Translation, pages 15–22
September 5, 2023, Macau SAR, China.

China were trained from childhood to guarantee high proficiency in the language. Similar cases appeared following the footsteps of Xuanzang (Felbur, 2022;Boucher, 1996) and Jesuit Figuists (Wei and Ling-chia, 2019) Finally, there stands the flood of translations from European languages and Japanese which served as a conduit for technical knowledge (and much else) following the Industrial Revolution.

In our own time, the leaps forward in Artificial Intelligence and Machine Learning development propels the rapid evolution of translation from a purely human activity to a machine-regulated one (Sommerschield et al, 2023). Indeed, Machine Translation may be the perfect solution to the problem that some target languages are less popular or difficult to learn (e.g. Classical Chinese) (Chang, 2021). However, the limited corpus, polysemy idiosyncrasy and complex semantic shifts when compared to Mandarin Chinese (Yang et al., 2020) pose significant hurdles to further developments in this area.

2. Related Work

Researchers have been working on Machine Translation at a feverish pace aroused by Neural Machine Translation (NMT) models like the transformer-based BERT in 2018 (Luong, 2016) which outperformed the former Recurrent Neural Network (RNN) and achieved astonishing success in Natural Language Processing (NLP) applications, including text understanding and thus Machine Translation (Rogers et al., 2020). Later, Liu et al (2019) released the more advanced derivative RoBERTa, which exceeded BERT thanks to its larger batch size, longer training process, dynamic masking pattern and so on, boosting its abilities in contextualized word processing and offering the potential of model fine-tuning. While optimizing general application of self-attention mechanism and neural network algorithm in Machine Translation (Qin, 2022), researchers also work to introduce models specialized for particular domain, such as the Siku-RoBERTa used in our study, which is pre-trained on "Siku Quanshu" for Classical Chinese-related translation (Tang, 2022). Other efforts were also paid for the Classical Chinese translation quality. For instance, Zhang et al (2022) developed an unsupervised algorithm to overcome the lack of sentence-aligned corpora, while another study adopted a distant-supervision-based method to solve the people name recognition issue in machine translation and other tasks (Zhang et al, 2021). In this paper, we describe a translation model developed on limited training datasets and pre-trained RoBERTa-based models. We apply this method both to the problem of Classical Chinese to Mandarin Chinese translation and Modern English translation. This allows us a comparative view of the impact of the training dataset size and other variables across languages.

3. Model

3.1 Key Features of the Model

Machine Translation is a sequence to sequence task which is usually trained by an encoder-decoder model. The input sequence is firstly passed through the encoder, which generates a contextualized representation for each input token. These representations are then passed to the decoder, which generates the output sequence. Siku-RoBERTa has 109M parameters and 50,265 vocabularies (Wang, 2022), while RoBERTa has 355M parameters and 29,791 vocabularies (Liu, 2019). We decided to use RoBERTa to be both encoder and decoder as it has more parameters and vocabularies which can generate a more detailed output. Compared with Siku-RoBERTa as encoder and RoBERTa as decoder, the decoder can understand more when the contextualized representation is generated by the same model. Meanwhile, training cost can be reduced by using shared encoder-decoder technique, it can reduce the memory usage from 109M+355M=464M parameters to 355M parameters.

3.2 Tokenizer

We used the Siku-RoBERTa tokenizer to tokenize input (Classical Chinese) and RoBERTa for output (English). In table 1, we demonstrate that both tokenizers can effectively decrease the number of tokens in their pretrained languages. Theoretically, they have a better interpretation in their own language, which is important when considering the maximum tokens input and output length of a model. When the length is too high, it will increase the computation cost as more tokens are trained and generated in each sentence. Table 1 shows that the average of token length is below 100. Therefore, choosing 192 as length can reduce computation cost without losing too much information from long sentences.

Data\Tokenizer	Siku_RoBERTa	RoBERTa
Total Input's tokens (Average)	160726 (27)	347764 (59)
Max No. of Input's	254	512
Total Output's tokens (Average)	374169 (64)	253175 (43)
Max No. of Output's	544	370

Table1

However, the tokenizers use different tokenization schemes and have different special token_ids. For example, Siku-RoBERTa uses 101 as [CLS] while RoBERTa uses 0 as [CLS]. This discrepancy might slightly affect the outcome of the training, so we decided to change the special tokens of Siku-RoBERTa to RoBERTa's in the input.

4. Experiment

4.1 English Model

4.1.1 Data

The EvaHan2023 competition provided 5,899 sentences of training data, about 160 thousand Chinese characters and 1 million English characters. Considering the data size is small, we preferred to train the whole dataset rather than splitting them into training and validation data. In spite of the risk of overfitting, a small dataset had a bigger effect on outcome.

4.1.2 Training

We considered two possible approaches:

Approach 1: Splitting data into training data (90%) and validation data (10%).

Approach 2: 100% training data and use 20% of training data as validation data.

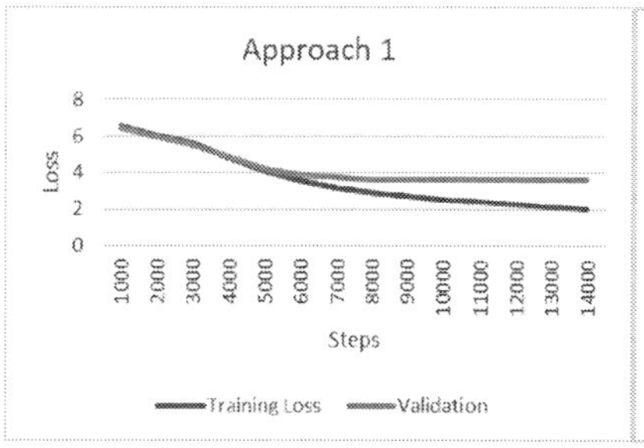

Figure 1

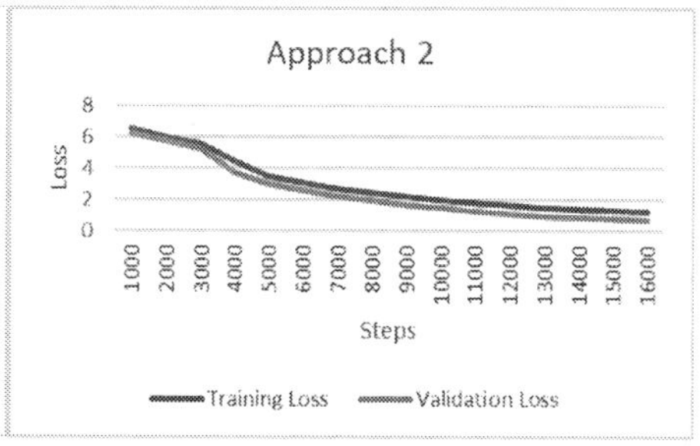

Figure 2

Approach 1 overfitted when the validation loss was around 3.6. Therefore, we used it as reference to predict the time model overfitted in Approach 2. We used a shared encoder-decoder model to lower the complexity of the model. Training Parameters: Learning rate=1.5e-5, Batch_size=8, Tie_encoder_decoder = true, epochs=20

4.1.3 Comparison

To investigate the relationship between data size and model performance, we also trained a model for translating from Classical Chinese to Mandarin Chinese. To keep it similar with the English model, we used Siku-RoBERTa as both the encoder and decoder. For the tokenizer, we used Siku-RoBERTa to tokenize input (Classical Chinese) and Chinese-RoBERTa_ wwm_ext for output (Mandarin Chinese). The model maximum output length was 192. We used two approaches to process training data for better comparison.

Approach 1 : Using the English model's dataset. The dataset was splitted to 5,309 (90%) for training and 590 (10%) for validation.

Approach 2 : Using the Chinese model's dataset. The dataset was splitted to 305,957 (99.5%) for training and 1,537 (0.5%) for validation. A smaller proportion of validation data was used to shorten the training time.

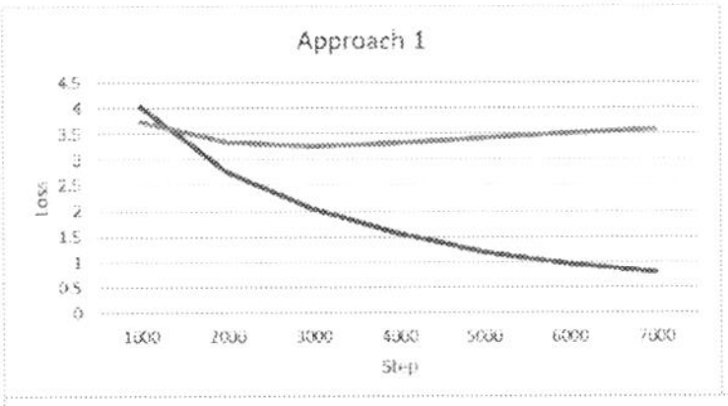

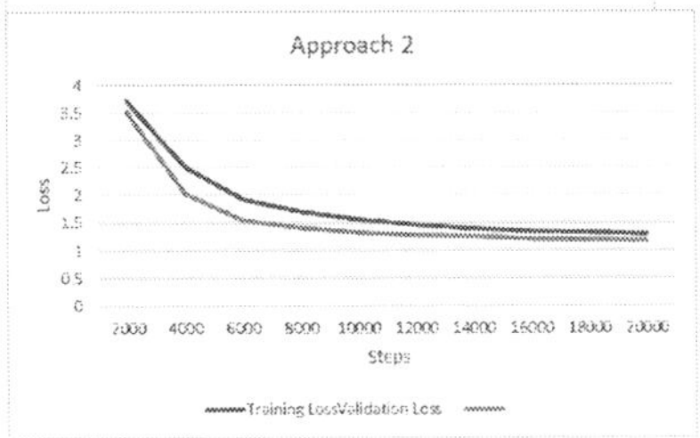

Figure 3 Figure 4

From figure 3, the Chinese model with small data size also resulted in overfit when validation loss is around 3.3. Comparing the score in table 2, we could see the Chinese model worked better than the English model when the data size was small. However, both of them resulted in a much worse performance than the model with larger datasets. It shows the importance of maximizing data size to train a good model.

Model	EN Approach 1/ EN Approach 2	M Approach 1	M Approach 2
BLEU	6.1	9.0	45.4
chrF	0.005	0.20	0.64

Table 2

4.2 Mandarin Chinese Model

4.2.1 Data and Model Architecture

During the experiment, the model was built on the Siku-RoBERTa model. The input was a sequence of Classical Chinese words, encoded using a WordPiece tokenizer. The encoded tokens were then input into the model, which generated a series of hidden states for each token. The final hidden state of the [CLS] token was used for translation. The model contained 9,583,749 characters of Classical Chinese text and 12,763,534 characters in the translation into Mandarin Chinese.

The output sequence was generated using a beam search algorithm, which considered multiple candidate solutions at each step to find the most probable output. The model was trained using the Adam optimizer with a learning rate of 1e-5 for 15 epochs, where batch_size was 16.

4.2.2 Experiments and Results

The experiments conducted on the model aimed to evaluate its performance in the task of translating Classical Chinese to Mandarin Chinese. The dataset was split into training and validation sets, with a 90-10 split ratio.

The first experiment involved training the model on the training set and evaluating its performance on the validation set. The experimental results showed that the Validation Loss of the model could reach as low as 0.0078, and it achieved a BLEU score of 37.8 and a chrF score of 0.47 on the validation set.

The second experiment involved using the trained model to translate a test dataset consisting of Classical Chinese texts. The model used in this experiment was the best-performing training model from the first experiment, and was used to generate Mandarin Chinese translations for the test dataset using a beam search algorithm. We chose the Mandarin Chinese translations provided by Google Translate as the reference translation, achieving a BLEU score of 32.1 and a chrF score of 0.33.

Experiment No.	1	2
BLEU	37.8	32.1
chrF	0.47	0.33

Table 3

5. Limitation

In the English translation model, it is clear that the dataset is too small, which restricts the model learning ability. Many words in the test data are untrained and data argumentation cannot help solve this problem.

In the experiments on Classical Chinese and Mandarin Chinese translation models, we found that the BLEU score cannot accurately reflect the performance of the translation model because the same content can be expressed using different words, which greatly affects the credibility of the BLEU score as a quality evaluation metric for translation. Future research directions may focus on finding more reliable scoring methods.

6. Conclusion

In sum, we used the RoBERTa model to train the Classical Chinese to English translation model, and the Siku-RoBERTa model to train Classical Chinese to Mandarin Chinese model. After comparing the result with the Mandarin Chinese model, we found that the dataset for the English model is too small for obtaining good results. Therefore, we further looked into the Mandarin Chinese model. The Siku-RoBERTa is fine-tuned for the specific task of translation and achieves a reasonable BLEU score on the validation and test datasets. The experiments conducted on the model demonstrate the effectiveness of the Siku-RoBERTa pre-trained model for NLP tasks and highlight the importance of pre-training on large datasets for achieving state-of-the-art performance. The results of the experiments show that the model has the potential to be used for practical translation applications.

References

Boucher, D. J. (1996). *Buddhist translation procedures in third-century China: a study of Dharmarakṣa and his translation idiom.* University of Pennsylvania.

Chang, K. (Kevin), Grafton, A., & Most, G. W. (2021). Recovering Translation Lost: Symbiosis and Ambilingual Design in Chinese/Manchu Language Reference Manuals of the Qing Dynasty. In *Impagination - Layout and Materiality of Writing and Publication* (pp. 323–350). Walter de Gruyter GmbH. https://doi.org/10.1515/9783110698756-012

Felbur, R., Meelen, M., & Vierthaler, P. (2022). Crosslinguistic Semantic Textual Similarity of Buddhist Chinese and Classical Tibetan. *Journal of Open Humanities Data, 8.*

Green, N. (2019). The Uses of Persian in Imperial China: Translating Practices at the Ming Court. In *The Persianate World* (pp. 113–130). University of California Press. https://doi.org/10.1515/9780520972100-007

Hung, E. (2005). Cultural borderlands in China's translation history. *Translation and cultural change: Studies in history, norms, and image projection, 61,* 43-64.

Liu, Y., Ott, M., Goyal, N., Du, J., Joshi, M., Chen, D., ... & Stoyanov, V. (2019). Roberta: A robustly optimized bert pretraining approach. *arXiv preprint arXiv:1907.11692.*

Luong, M. T. (2016). *Neural machine translation* (Doctoral dissertation, Stanford University).

Qin, Q. (2022). Design and application of Chinese English machine translation model based on improved bidirectional neural network fusion attention mechanism. *Wireless Communications and Mobile Computing, 2022.*

Rogers, A., Kovaleva, O., & Rumshisky, A. (2021). A primer in BERTology: What we know about how BERT works. *Transactions of the Association for Computational Linguistics, 8*, 842-866.

Sommerschield, T., Assael, Y., Pavlopoulos, J., Stefanak, V., Senior, A., Dyer, C., ... & de Freitas, N. (2023). Machine Learning for Ancient Languages: A Survey. *Computational Linguistics*, 1-44.

Tang, B., Lin, B., & Li, S. (2022, June). Simple Tagging System with RoBERTa for Ancient Chinese. In *Proceedings of the Second Workshop on Language Technologies for Historical and Ancient Languages* (pp. 159-163).

王東波, 劉暢, 朱子赫, 劉江峰, 胡昊天, & 沈思等. (2022). Sikubert 與 sikuroberta:面向數字人文的《四庫全書》預訓練模型構建及應用研究(pp.7).圖書館論壇.

Wei, S. L. (2019). *Chinese theology and translation : the Christianity of the Jesuit figurists and their Christianized Yijing.* Routledge.

Yang, K., Liu, D., Qu, Q., Sang, Y., & Lv, J. (2021). An automatic evaluation metric for Ancient-Modern Chinese translation. Neural Computing and Applications, 33, 3855-3867.

Zhang, H., Zhu, H., Ruan, J., & Ding, R. (2021, May). People name recognition from ancient Chinese literature using distant supervision and deep learning. In *2021 2nd International Conference on Artificial Intelligence and Information Systems* (pp. 1-6).

Zhang, Z., Li, W., & Su, Q. (2019). Automatic translating between ancient Chinese and contemporary Chinese with limited aligned corpora. In *Natural Language Processing and Chinese Computing: 8th CCF International Conference, NLPCC 2019, Dunhuang, China, October 9–14, 2019, Proceedings, Part II 8* (pp. 157-167). Springer International Publishing.

Pre-trained Model In Ancient-Chinese-to-Modern-Chinese Machine Translation

Jiahui Wang wangjiahui@smail.nju.edu.cn
Xuqin Zhang 2580334082@qq.com
Kuangyaming Honor School, Nanjing University, Nanjing, 210023, China

Jiahuan Li lijh@smail.nju.edu.cn
Shujian Huang huangsj@nju.edu.cn
National Key Laboratory for Novel Software Technology, Nanjing University, Nanjing, 210023, China

Abstract

Neural Machine Translation (NMT) has emerged as a powerful approach for language translation, with the Transformer model revolutionizing the field. One key aspect that has propelled the Transformer's success is the utilization of pre-training techniques. This paper presents an analysis of the pre-trained Transformer model NMT for the Ancient-Chinese-to-Modern-Chinese machine translation task.

1 Introduction

The Transformer model (Vaswani et al., 2017) has demonstrated exceptional performance in various natural language processing tasks, including machine translation. One key aspect that has propelled the Transformer's success is the utilization of pre-training techniques, such as the popular BERT (Devlin et al., 2018) model. By pre-training on large-scale corpora, BERT captures rich linguistic representations and context, allowing for more effective transfer learning.

In this study, we incorporate a pre-trained Transformer model, Chinese-RoBERTa-wwm-ext (Cui et al., 2021) into our NMT system, enabling it to leverage the wealth of linguistic knowledge encoded in the pre-training process. By fine-tuning the pre-trained model on translation-specific data, we aim to exploit the benefits of both pre-training and task-specific learning.

2 Related Work

The currently most commonly used BERT model (Devlin et al., 2018) is pre-trained on general-domain text using universal language representation. While the model exhibits strong generality, its performance is easily constrained when applied to natural language processing tasks involving domain-specific texts. Due to the inherent differences in grammar, semantics, and pragmatics between Ancient Chinese and other languages, there are significant deviations in features. It is challenging to achieve the same performance level as in general corpora. Therefore, the direct application of BERT in projects related to Ancient Chinese does not yield ideal results.

Proceedings of ALT2023: First Workshop on Ancient Language Translation, pages 23–28
September 5, 2023, Macau SAR, China.

AnchiBERT (Tian et al., 2021) is a pre-trained model specifically designed for Ancient Chinese texts. It "reads" a total of 39.5 million characters of Ancient Chinese, including historical records, prose, ancient poetry, and couplets, spanning thousands of years. The downstream tasks of AnchiBERT include comprehension and generation of Ancient Chinese texts. The paper suggests that to use AnchiBERT for text generation in Ancient Chinese, a framework based on the Transformer model can be adopted. The encoder part of the framework utilizes AnchiBERT, while the decoder part uses the original Transformer model's decoder with randomly initialized parameters.

In the same year, Dongbo Wang et al. employed high-quality, validated full-text corpus from the Qing Dynasty's Qianlong period edition of the extensive series "Siku Quanshu" as an unsupervised training set. They continued training a BERT model based on the BERT structure, incorporating a large amount of Ancient Chinese texts. This led to the development of the Siku BERT (Wang et al., 2022) pre-trained language model specifically tailored for intelligent processing tasks related to Ancient Chinese. By directly using the pre-trained model as initialization parameters, not only did the model possess stronger generalization capabilities and faster convergence speed, but it also required only a small amount of labeled data for fine-tuning, significantly improving the performance of natural language processing tasks while avoiding overfitting.

The Siku BERT pre-trained language model and AnchiBERT pre-trained model introduced the idea of transfer learning in low-resource machine translation research. This can provide a theoretical and practical foundation for the text generation project in Ancient Chinese.

3 Approach

We employed a standard Transformer-based NMT architecture with the pre-trained model, Chinese-RoBERTa-wwm-ext (Cui et al., 2021) as the encoder and a randomly initialized decoder, depicted in Figure 1 .Chinese-RoBERTa-wwm-ext(Cui et al., 2021), as an advanced language model specifically designed for processing and understanding the Chinese language, has demonstrated exceptional performance on a wide range of Chinese NLP benchmarks, surpassing previous state-of-the-art models in tasks such as text classification, sentiment analysis, and natural language understanding. During the training process, we employed a strategy where the encoder parameters were frozen, and only the decoder parameters were updated. At the same time, we adopted the technology of joined dictionary. Thanks to the similarity between Ancient Chinese and Modern Chinese, joined vocabulary simplifies the process of aligning words between Ancient Chinese and Modern Chinese. By using a joined dictionary, identical words only require one embedding vector, reducing the number of model parameters, memory consumption, and computational overhead, thereby enhancing training efficiency.

4 Experinental Setup

Data: The source of the training data includes the Ancient-Chinese-to-Modern-Chinese parallel texts of China Twenty-four Histories, with 9,583,749 characters for the original Ancient Chinese texts as source data and 12,763,534 characters modern Chinese translation as target data.

Training Details: The model was implemented on the top of fairseq toolkit[1]. The dropout rate was set to 0.3. We set weight decay to $1e-4$ to overcome over-fitting. We used Adam (Kingma and Ba, 2014) to optimize the model parameters, with $\beta_1 = 0.9$ and $\beta_2 = 0.98$.

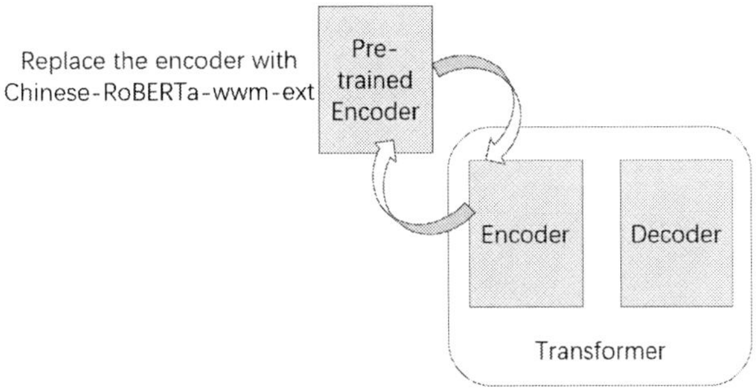

Figure 1: Model Architecture

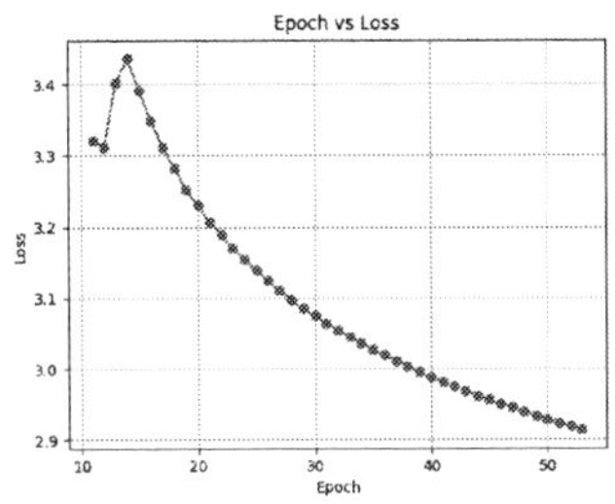

(a) Loss

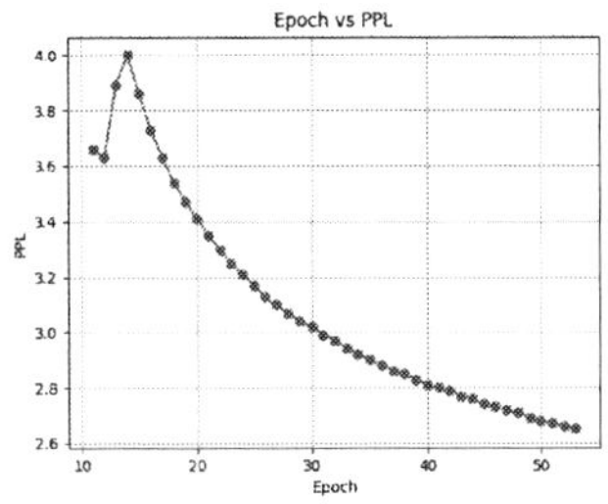

(b) PPL

Figure 2: Loss and PPL

5 Results

During local test, we get the following results. Figure 1 shows the loss during training and the change of perplexity(PPL), both of which decrease steadily. Figure 2 shows the changes in the BLEU (Papineni et al., 2002) score of the validation set, showing an upward trend. The performance on the valid set of the best checkpoint was evaluated with the following metrics: Loss: The overall loss achieved on the valid set was 3.192. Loss represents the discrepancy between the predicted output and the ground truth and is minimized during training. Negative Log-Likelihood (NLL) Loss: The NLL loss was calculated as 1.61. It measures the average negative log probability of the correct target tokens given the model's predictions. Perplexity (PPL): The perplexity value obtained was 3.05. PPL is a measure of how well the model predicts the next token in the sequence. Lower perplexity indicates better predictive performance. BLEU Score: The BLEU score achieved on the valid set was 35.84. BLEU is a widely used metric to evaluate the quality of machine translation outputs. A higher BLEU score indicates better translation quality.

By integrating our translation examples, we have observed that our model can produce relatively smooth translations for short sentences. While some individual words may not be translated directly into modern Chinese, this does not hinder the conveyance of meaning, as depicted in Figure 4. However, in Figure 5, the model struggles to accurately analyze pronouns

[1]https://github.com/facebookresearch/fairseq

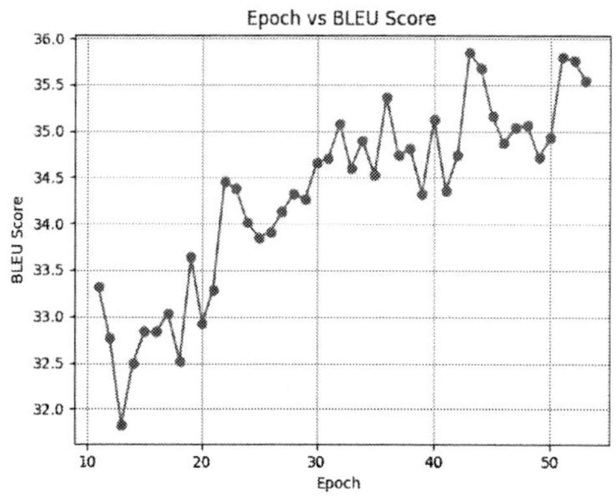

Figure 3: BLEU on valid set

Ancient:復劾罷江西巡撫韓光祐。（简体：复劾罢江西巡抚韩光祐）

Reference:又揭發罷免江西巡撫韓光祐。（简体：又揭发罢免江西巡抚韩光祐）

Hypothesis:又彈劾罷免江西巡撫韓光祐。（简体：又弹劾罢免江西巡抚韩光祐）

Figure 4: Short example1

that require expansion based on context. Although this does not significantly impact the overall comprehension of the translated sentences, it does emphasize the importance of incorporating longer contextual information. For short sentences, relying solely on the source-to-target sentence pairs may not suffice to effectively translate referential information.

For longer sentences, as shown in Figure 6, we have found that our model is generally able to maintain consistency in conveying meaning. Although the accuracy of the translation may slightly decrease with increasing sentence length, there are instances where certain vocabulary may not be rendered with utmost precision. Nonetheless, overall comprehension of the sentences can still be achieved. On some vocabulary, our model translates more detail. Also, the model demonstrates a high level of proficiency in accurately recognizing and classifying proper nouns. Its advanced language processing capabilities enable it to effectively identify and distinguish names of specific people, places, organizations, and other entities.

In the official EvaHan2023[2] test set, the best model achieves the BLEU score of 22.05.

[2]https://github.com/GoThereGit/EvaHan

Ancient: 其子孫年幼者咸配流嶺外，誅其親黨數百餘家。（简体：其子孙年幼者咸配流岭外，诛其亲党数百馀家。）

Reference: 他們的子孫年幼的都流放嶺外，誅殺他們的親黨幾百家。（简体：他们的子孙年幼的都流放岭外，诛杀他们的亲党几百家）

Hypothesis: 其子孫年幼的都流放到嶺外，誅殺其親黨數百多家。（简体：其子孙年幼的都流放到岭外，诛杀其亲党数百多家。）

Figure 5: Short example2

Ancient：五年正月己丑，詔立之：“凡為小吳決口所立堤防，可按視河勢向背應置埽處，毋虛設巡河官，毋橫費工料。

Reference：五年正月己丑，詔令李立之：“凡為小吳決口所立的堤防，可視察河勢向背及應設埽處，不要虛設巡河官員，不要浪費工料。

Hypothesis：五年正月己丑，詔令設立：凡是被小吳決口所設立的堤防，可以考察河勢向背，應設置的地方，不要虛設巡河官，不要隨意花費工料。

(a)

Ancient：十月丙子朔，詔張俊援世忠，劉光世移軍建康。世忠復還揚州。起張浚為侍讀。戊子，韓世忠戰於大儀，己丑，解元戰於承州，皆捷。

Reference：十月丙子初一，詔命張俊救援韓世忠，劉光世移兵到建康。韓世忠又回到揚州。起用張浚為侍讀。戊子，韓世忠戰於大儀，己丑，解元戰於承州，都獲勝。

Hypothesis：十月丙子初一，詔令張俊援助韓世忠，劉光世移軍建康。韓世忠又回到揚州。起用張浚為侍讀。戊子，韓世忠在大儀交戰，己丑，解元在承州交戰，都獲勝。

(b)

Figure 6: Translation examples sampled from validation set

6 Conclusion

In this study, we explored the application of pre-trained Transformer models in Ancient-Chinese-to-Modern-Chinese machine translation. By incorporating the Chinese-RoBERTa-wwm-ext model as the encoder in our NMT system, we aimed to leverage the rich linguistic representations and contextual knowledge captured through pre-training. Our findings and experimental results shed light on the effectiveness of pre-training techniques for improving translation quality in this specific language pair. By leveraging pre-training techniques and adopting a joined dictionary approach, we achieved moderately satisfactory results, exploring the way for Ancient-Chinese-to-Modern-Chinese machine translation.

References

Cui, Y., Che, W., Liu, T., Qin, B., and Yang, Z. (2021). Pre-training with whole word masking for chinese bert.

Devlin, J., Chang, M.-W., Lee, K., and Toutanova, K. (2018). Bert: Pre-training of deep bidirectional transformers for language understanding. *arXiv preprint arXiv:1810.04805*.

Kingma, D. P. and Ba, J. (2014). Adam: A method for stochastic optimization. *arXiv preprint arXiv:1412.6980*.

Papineni, K., Roukos, S., Ward, T., and Zhu, W.-J. (2002). Bleu: a method for automatic evaluation of machine translation. In *Proceedings of the 40th annual meeting of the Association for Computational Linguistics*, pages 311–318.

Tian, H., Yang, K., Liu, D., and Lv, J. (2021). Anchibert: A pre-trained model for ancient chinese language understanding and generation. In *2021 International Joint Conference on Neural Networks (IJCNN)*, pages 1–8. IEEE.

Vaswani, A., Shazeer, N., Parmar, N., Uszkoreit, J., Jones, L., Gomez, A. N., Kaiser, Ł., and Polosukhin, I. (2017). Attention is all you need. *Advances in neural information processing systems*, 30.

Wang, D., Liu, C., Zhu, Z., Liu, J., Hu, H., Shen, S., and Li, B. (2022). Sikubert and sikuroberta: Construction and application research of pretrained models for digital humanities in siku quanshu. *Library Tribune*, 42(6):31–43.

Some Trials on Ancient Modern Chinese Translation

Li Lin efsotr_l@stu.pku.edu.cn.Peking University.China
Xinyu Hu huxinyu@pku.edu.cn.Peking University.China

Abstract

In this study, we explored various neural machine translation techniques for the task of translating ancient Chinese into modern Chinese. Our aim was to find an effective method for achieving accurate and reliable translation results. After experimenting with different approaches, we discovered that the method of concatenating adjacent sentences yielded the best performance among all the methods tested.

1 Introduction

Chinese characters are the writing system of Chinese and are considered one of the oldest written languages in the world. According to verifiable records, over 3000 years ago, Chinese characters had already developed a mature writing system, including oracle bone inscriptions. While some characters have been retained throughout the subsequent development process, the expression forms and meanings of ancient Chinese and modern Chinese differ significantly. Ancient Chinese often features rare words that are not commonly found in modern Chinese, and the grammar structures also vary. Consequently, reading ancient Chinese poses difficulties for modern individuals, often necessitating the expertise of professionals to translate it into modern Chinese.

Neural Machine Translation has already demonstrated remarkable performance in various bilingual translation tasks. However, there has been limited exploration of the existing advanced Neural Machine Translation technology in the domain of monolingual translation from ancient Chinese to modern Chinese. This relatively specialized field has received little attention in terms of developing Neural Machine Translation technology. In this Evahan 2023 competition, we are participating in the task of translating ancient Chinese into modern Chinese. The training data of this task is extracted from the Twenty-Four Histories (recording the history from the pre Qin period to the Ming Dynasty), which was finished by the research group of the National Social Science Foundation of China major project "Research on the Construction and Application of Cross-language Knowledge Base of Ancient Chinese Classics" (project No. :21&ZD331)

In this paper, we begin by introducing the methods employed in our study, including data augmentation, fine-tuning of pre-trained models, and attention mechanisms such as group attention. Next, we provide details on our training setting, including the use of pre-trained models, data segmentation, vocabulary construction, and the division of training and validation sets. We also present the experimental results, including the performance of different methods on evaluation metrics such as BLEU and ChrF. Lastly, we discuss the outcomes of our attempts, highlighting the effectiveness of certain techniques, the limitations of others, and the potential for further improvements in low-resource translation tasks.

Proceedings of ALT2023: First Workshop on Ancient Language Translation, pages 29–33
September 5, 2023, Macau SAR, China.

2 Method

In this section, we will describe some methods that we have tried.

Data augmentation Data augmentation is an essential technique in machine learning tasks to increase the size and diversity of the training data. In our case, we have observed that adjacent sentences in the training data are typically in the same article. Therefore, a straightforward data augmentation method we employ is concatenating adjacent sentences to form longer sentences. We denote the concatenation of no more than k sentences as k-cat.

Tune Training translation models can be seen as training classification models, as both tasks involve categorizing text. However, the challenge arises from the presence of numerous categories, leading to a long tail problem. To address this issue, we draw inspiration from the approach described in (Menon et al., 2020).

In our methodology, we augment the trained model by adding $\log P(x)$ to the bias term of the final classification layer. Here, $P(x)$ represents the prior distribution of token x, which is derived from the distribution observed in the training set. Subsequently, we continue training the model, while keeping the non-classification layers frozen.

Group attention Group attention techniques (Bao et al., 2021), such as group attention and combine attention, were applied to data augmented with concatenated sentences. Group attention focuses exclusively on information within the same sentence during attention calculations, while combine attention combines group attention with traditional global attention.

Finetune pre-trained model To further enhance the model's performance, we conducted fine-tuning using the Masked LM technique inspired by BERT (Devlin et al., 2018). The pre-trained model was trained for 50 epochs on the training dataset. Subsequently, the fine-tuned model was loaded and trained on the 3-cat and 4-cat data.

3 Experiment

3.1 Baseline setting

For the translation model, we utilize the encoder-decoder Transformer architecture (Vaswani et al., 2017) and employ the EncoderDecoderModel which is provided by the Hugging Face library [1] to build our system. The basic model loads the first 6 layers of SikuBERT (Wang et al., 2022) (resp. Chinese-BERT-wwm (Cui et al., 2020)) parameters for encoder (resp. decoder) part. In the embedding layer of encoder (resp. decoder), the corresponding parameters are loaded for the original tokens (resp. the original simplified tokens), and if unavailable, the [UNK] parameters are used. The remaining parameters in the model are initialized randomly.

3.2 Training detail

For all experiments, we adopt the AdamW optimizer (Loshchilov and Hutter, 2017). The hyper parameters of AdamW optimizer set as follows : $\beta_1 = 0.9, \beta_2 = 0.999, \epsilon = 1e-8, \lambda = 0.01$. The learning rate is scheduled using inverse_sqrt with a maximum learning rate of 1.5e-4 and warmup steps of 30000. We set the label smoothing as 0.1 and the batch size as 32. For the Tune method, we set the maximum learning rate to 4e-5 and the warmup steps to 10000. We use beam search with beam size 5 for decoding and report the BLEU score (Papineni et al., 2002) and the ChrF score (Popović, 2015) on validation set.

During our experiments, we observed that after training for 4 to 7 epochs, the validation set loss would start to increase. However, during this time, the BLEU and ChrF scores of

[1] `https://huggingface.co/`

the validation set continued to improve. So, our stopping strategy is based on the validation set's BLEU score: if it does not exceed the highest point for five consecutive epochs, we stop training. After stopping, we select the checkpoint with the highest BLEU score among the last five epochs or their average as the final training result.

3.3 Data preprocess and vocabulary

Brief overview of training data The training data comprises around 0.3 million parallel corpora, encompassing both ancient Chinese and modern Chinese texts. In the training data, ancient Chinese has been supplemented with modern punctuation marks. An important point to note is that both ancient Chinese and modern Chinese are written using traditional Chinese characters.

Data preprocess The training data undergoes several processing steps. To handle sentences that exceed the length of 256 tokens, we first segment them based on the ending punctuation marks. In order to align the segmented portions, we utilize a similarity metric based on 1-gram, 2-gram, and 3-gram comparisons. To determine the optimal alignment scheme, we employ dynamic programming techniques. This helps us align the segments in a way that maximizes the similarity between the original and translated texts while ensuring that the segments do not exceed the maximum length limit of 256 tokens. However, some segments may still surpass the 256-length limit or exhibit significant length discrepancies between the original and translated texts. These segments, representing either non-translatable sections or incorrect training data alignment, are discarded.

The training set and validation set are randomly divided in a 9:1 ratio. Then, based on the training set, we generate k-cat data by concatenating adjacent sentences, as described in section 2. The statistics of the training, k-cat, and validation sets, including the number of sentences and characters, are presented in Table 1.

	baseline	2-cat	3-cat	4-cat	valid
#sents	320K	584K	801K	980K	36K
#src chars	8M	21M	36M	53M	0.89M
#tgt chars	10M	27M	48M	69M	1.2M

Table 1: Number of sentences and characters in training, k-cat, and validation sets.

Vocabulary The word segmentation method used in this task is based on single characters. When constructing the vocabulary, we consider only those words that appear more than 5 times in the training set. The dictionary sizes for the encoder and decoder can be seen in table 2.

	#vocab(occur $\geq$ 6)	#vocab
src	6,367	9,425
tgt	5,997	8,548

Table 2: Dictionary Sizes for Ancient and Modern Chinese

4 Result & Discussion

The results of the experiments are presented in table 3. It can be observed that as the number of concatenated sentences increases, the performance of the model improves. However, there is a diminishing return effect, and the performance essentially plateaus at 4-cat.

Method	baseline	2-cat	3-cat	4-cat	3-cat(tune)	4-cat(tune)
BLEU	61.451*	63.386	63.728	63.838*	63.824	**63.941**
ChrF	58.986*	61.186	61.561	61.696*	61.651	**61.774**

Table 3: Performance comparison of baseline and k-cat models, where k ranges from 2 to 4. The table also includes the performance of 3-cat and 4-cat models that were tuned without modifying the bias. Note: * indicates that the result is the average of multiple checkpoints.

We have also experimented with alternative initial embedding parameter methods, such as integrating the embedding of ancient and modern parts and incorporating additional dictionary definitions. However, these methods did not yield significant improvements in performance. In fact, in some cases, these alternative methods even resulted in worse results. As a result, we concluded that the current initial embedding parameter approach, as described earlier, is the most suitable for our task.

For the tune method, we have found that the performance of the model remains comparable even after removing these modifications and training the model using the same settings. Furthermore, after applying the tune method, there is a slight improvement in BLEU score of approximately 0.1. Similarly, the ChrF metric shows a slight improvement of less than 0.1. These improvements indicate that the tuning process has a positive impact on the model's translation quality, albeit with modest gains.

For the group attention method, our experiments involved testing different learning rates. However, the results consistently showed that this method resulted in significantly worse performance compared to the standard attention method. In this particular setting, this indicates that either using group attention limits the model's capability or that training the model with this method requires careful adjustment of learning rates across all model components. It is possible that the introduction of group attention affects the gradients differently, making the learning process more sensitive and challenging. Therefore, further investigation and fine-tuning of the model's learning rates would be necessary to achieve better performance with the group attention method.

For the fine-tune pre-trained model method, the results showed an improvement of approximately 0.06 in BLEU and 0.07 in ChrF for the 3-cat data. However, there was no improvement observed for the 4-cat data, which can be attributed to the lower performance after the average checkpoint. The reason for the limited improvement in this method is likely due to the small size of the fine-tuning data. With a small amount of data available for fine-tuning, the model may not have sufficient exposure to the specific characteristics and patterns of the task at hand.

5 Conclusion

In conclusion, among all the methods explored in our experiments, the data augmentation technique of directly concatenating sentences proved to be the most effective. However, as the number of concatenated sentences increased, the improvement in performance became less significant. This suggests that simply adding more repetitive data does not necessarily lead to better results. It also indicates that the potential of the model may not be fully utilized with only 0.3M parallel sentences. Therefore, for low-resource translation tasks such as translating from ancient Chinese to modern Chinese, data augmentation methods should be the primary approach to consider.

References

Bao, G., Zhang, Y., Teng, Z., Chen, B., and Luo, W. (2021). G-transformer for document-level machine translation. In *Proceedings of the 59th Annual Meeting of the Association for Computational Linguistics and the 11th International Joint Conference on Natural Language Processing (Volume 1: Long Papers)*, pages 3442–3455, Online. Association for Computational Linguistics.

Cui, Y., Che, W., Liu, T., Qin, B., Wang, S., and Hu, G. (2020). Revisiting pre-trained models for Chinese natural language processing. In *Proceedings of the 2020 Conference on Empirical Methods in Natural Language Processing: Findings*, pages 657–668, Online. Association for Computational Linguistics.

Devlin, J., Chang, M.-W., Lee, K., and Toutanova, K. (2018). Bert: Pre-training of deep bidirectional transformers for language understanding. *arXiv preprint arXiv:1810.04805*.

Loshchilov, I. and Hutter, F. (2017). Decoupled weight decay regularization. *arXiv preprint arXiv:1711.05101*.

Menon, A. K., Jayasumana, S., Rawat, A. S., Jain, H., Veit, A., and Kumar, S. (2020). Long-tail learning via logit adjustment. *arXiv preprint arXiv:2007.07314*.

Papineni, K., Roukos, S., Ward, T., and Zhu, W.-J. (2002). Bleu: a method for automatic evaluation of machine translation. In *Proceedings of the 40th annual meeting of the Association for Computational Linguistics*, pages 311–318.

Popović, M. (2015). chrf: character n-gram f-score for automatic mt evaluation. In *Proceedings of the tenth workshop on statistical machine translation*, pages 392–395.

Vaswani, A., Shazeer, N., Parmar, N., Uszkoreit, J., Jones, L., Gomez, A. N., Kaiser, Ł., and Polosukhin, I. (2017). Attention is all you need. *Advances in neural information processing systems*, 30.

Wang, D., Liu, C., Zhu, Z., LIU, J., HU, H., SHEN, S., and LI, B. (2022). Construction and application of pre-trained models of siku quanshu in orientation to digital humanities [j]. *Library Tribune*, 42(06):31–43.

Istic Neural Machine Translation System for EvaHan 2023

Ningyuan Deng dengny2022@istic.ac.cn
Shuao Guo guosa2021@istic.ac.cn
Yanqing He* heyq@istic.ac.cn
Research Center of Information Theory and Methodology, Institute of Scientific and Technical Information of China, Beijing 100038, China

Abstract

This paper presents the system architecture and the technique details adopted by Institute of Scientific and Technical Information of China (ISTIC) in the evaluation of First Conference on EvaHan(2023). In this evaluation, ISTIC participated in two tasks of Ancient Chinese Machine Translation: Ancient Chinese to Modern Chinese and Ancient Chinese to English. The paper mainly elaborates the model framework and data processing methods adopted in ISTIC's system. Finally a comparison and analysis of different machine translation systems are also given.

1. Introduction

This paper presents a detailed overview of the machine translation system of the Institute of Scientific and Technical Information of China (ISTIC) in the EvaHan (2023) evaluation task. ISTIC participated in the Ancient-Modern Chinese and Ancient-English translation tasks.In this evaluation Google Transformer[1] is used as the baseline system. Open source monolingual data is forward translated to construct a pseudo-parallel corpus to expand the training set released by EvaHan (2023) Evaluation side. Data pre-processing includes special character filtering, sentence de-duplication, length-ratio filtering and Pinyin coding. In the construction of the system model, a context-awareness-based approach[2] encode the context as an additional neural network. Then the model integration method are used to obtain the final translation results.

The structure of this paper is structured as follows: Section 2 introduces the system framework and technical approach adopted by ISTIC. Section 3 presents the experimental setting and results. Finally we conclude our work in Section 4.

---

[1] Vaswani, A., et al.: Attention is all you need. In: Advances in Neural Information Processing Systems 30 (NIPS 2017), pp. 5998 - 6008 (2017)

[2] Fernandes, P., Yin, K., Neubig, G., & Martins, A. F. T. (2018). Measuring and Increasing Context Usage in Context-Aware Machine Translation. In Proceedings of the 2018 Conference of the North American Chapter of the Association for Computational Linguistics: Human Language Technologies, Volume 1 (Long Papers) (pp. 1114-1123).

Proceedings of ALT2023: First Workshop on Ancient Language Translation, pages 34–42
September 5, 2023, Macau SAR, China.

2. System

ISTIC participated in Ancient-Modern Chinese task (a2m) and Ancient-English task (a2e). Figure 1 shows the system architecture of our machine translation including data augmentation, data preprocessing, data set partition, model training, model inference and data post-processing.

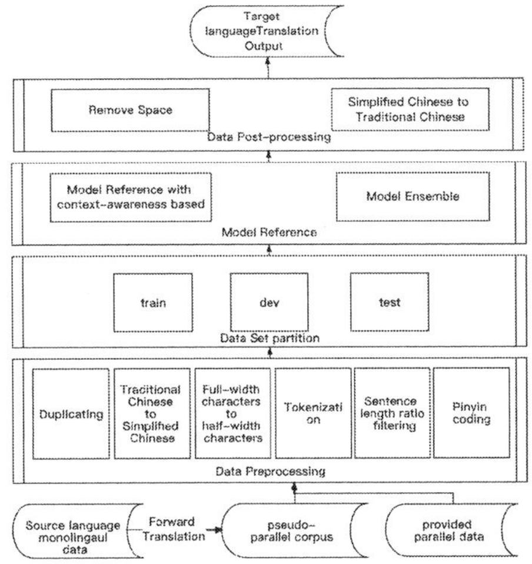

Figure 1:flow chart of our machine translation system

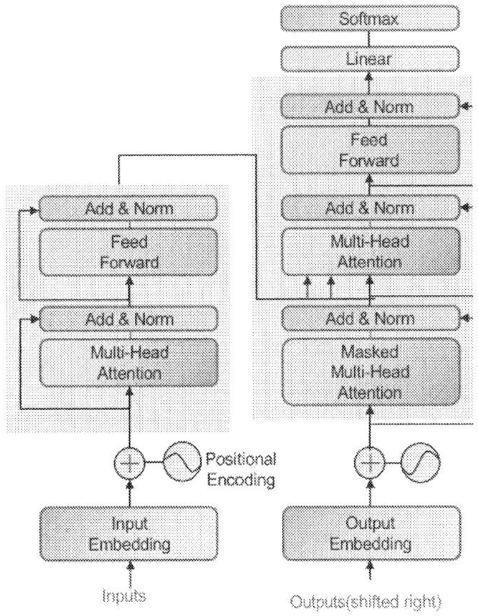

Figure 2:Transformer[2] model structure

2.1. Data augmentation

Forward translation is one of the common ways of data augmentation[3].We first train the translation models of a2m and a2e using the released data. Then ancient Chinese monolingual data is collected from internet and translated by the above two machine translation models to construct pseudo-bilingual pairs. Finally the released parallel sentence pairs are merged with pseudo-bilingual pairs as the final data.

2.2. Data Preprocessing

The main stages of preprocessing are as follows.

1. Duplicating:We remove repetitive sentences to reduce the training time of machine translation models
2. Traditional Chinese to Simplified Chinese: By converting traditional Chinese to simplified Chinese we can obtain a uniformly encoding for each same Chinese word.

[3] Nishant Kambhatla, Logan Born, and Anoop Sarkar. 2022. CipherDAug: Ciphertext based Data Augmentation for Neural Machine Translation. In Proceedings of the 60th Annual Meeting of the Association for Computational Linguistics (Volume 1: Long Papers), pages 201 – 218, Dublin, Ireland. Association for Computational Linguistics.

3. Full-width characters to half-width characters: Because full-width characters and half-width characters have different Unicode encoding, we converts full-width characters to half-width characters in order to avoid inconsistent rendering of text, or even garbled code.
4.Tokenization: We tokenize the data into meaningful units, so that the translation system can understand and process the input text more accurately and make the vocabulary smaller.
5. Sentence length ratio filtering: The sentence lengths ratio of the source language and target language can help to filter poor bilingual pairs.
6. Pinyin coding: Chinese characters may correspond to multiple pronunciations.So we converts Chinese characters into corresponding Pinyin coding in order to more accurately match the similarities and correlations between the source and target language.

2.3. Data Set Partition

We split all the preprocessed data into: a training set, a test set, and a validation set.The training set and the validation set are used to train the supervised machine translation model and adjust the parameters.The test set is employed to verify whether the trained model has the same effect in other data. The partition ratio of the dataset is train:test:dev=90:5:5.

2.4. Model Inference

Our system is based on Google Transformer[4]. As shown in Figure 2, Transformer comprises two components: an encoder layer (with self-attention and fully connected layers) and a decoder layer (with self-attention, encoder-decoder attention, and fully connected layers), and each of them consists of 6 modules. The model adopts the self-attention mechanism and realizes algorithm parallelism to improve translation quality.

The data of the evaluation tasks are all sentences pairs and lack contexts information. Therefore a context-awareness-based approach is employed and multi-encoder concatenate[5] the source sentence and their contexts, such as inside-context, outside-context and Gaussian noise context.

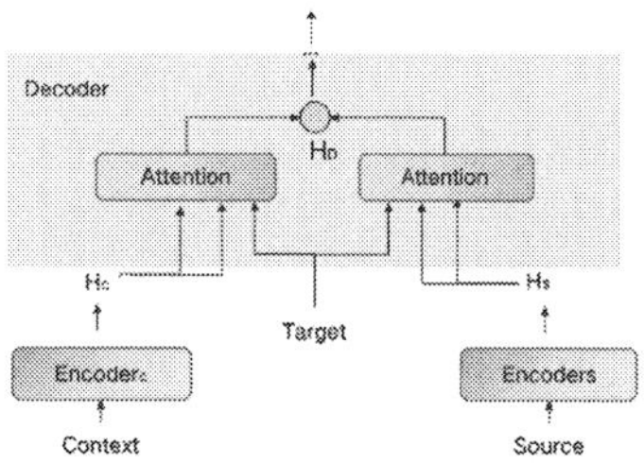

Figure 3. Inside-context method.

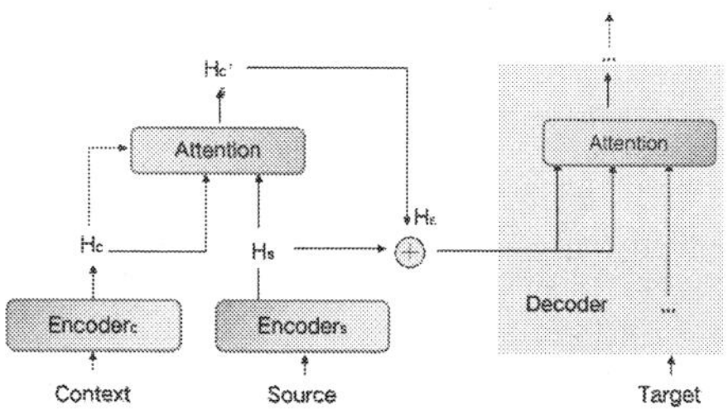

Figure 4 Outside-context method.

(1)Inside-context: We use Pinyin coding of source language or source language itself as its context.In a2m tasks,And Since ancient Chinese has kanji, homophones, supplemental Pinyin can pass kanji information .In a2e task ,Chinese characters does not make full use of the internal semantics of Chinese, while the Latin alphabet has prefix suffixes such as de and an. Therefore,

---

[4] Facebook Research. Fairseq: A Fast, Extensible Toolkit for Sequence Modeling. Github, 2016, https://github.com/facebookresearch/fairseq.
[5] Bei Li, Hui Liu, Ziyang Wang, Yufan Jiang, Tong Xiao, Jingbo Zhu, Tongran Liu, and Changliang Li. 2020. Does Multi-Encoder Help? A Case Study on Context-Aware Neural Machine Translation. In Proceedings of the 58th Annual Meeting of the Association for Computational Linguistics, pages 3512 - 3518, Online. Association for Computational Linguistics.

supplementing the Pinyin coding can make the correspondence with the Latin alphabet, so as to show more of the internal characteristics of Chinese characters, and establish a relationship with the English, so as to solve the problem of learning bottlenect and parameter bottlenect. As shown in Figure 3, firstly, the decoder can attend to two encoders respectively ,which are H_s (the hidden layer of source sentence)and H_c (the hidden state of the contexts).Then in decoder layer,we concat H_c and H_s with H_t (the hidden layer of target sentence) to form $H_{c'}$ and $H_{s'}$ .Finally the gating mechanism inside the decoder is employed to obtain H_D (the fusion vector). In the Inside approach, Target is the query, Hs and Hc represent key/value.

$$H_{c'} = Concat(H_c, H_t)$$

$$H_{s'} = Concat(H_s, H_t)$$

$$H_D = MultiHead(H_{c'}, H_{s'})$$

(2)Outside-context: We also use Pinyin coding of source language or source language as its context.As shown in Figure 4, firstly we convert current source sentence and its context into new vectors H_s (the hidden layer of source sentence)and H_c (the hidden state of the contexts) . Through the attention mechanism of the encoder,we concat H_c and H_s to form a new vector ,called $H_{c'}$(the hidden state of the attention part of the encoder). Then the attention output ($H_{c'}$) and the source sentence(H_s) are fused by a gated sum to form H_E(the mutihead encoder layer).. **In the Outside approach, Hs is the query and Hc is thekey/value.**

$$H_{c'} = Concat(H_c, H_s)$$

$$H_E = MutiHead(H_{c'} \quad H_s)$$

(3)Gaussian-noise-context:It is similar to outside-context method.It add Gaussian noise to the encoder output and combining the context with Gaussian noise.

2.5. Model ensemble

Model ensemble[6] can improve the generalization ability of the final model by fusing multiple trained models. Then ultimate result involves weighted average of probability distribution for predictions, which combines the learning capabilities of all the individual models

2.6. Data post-processing

In the Ancient Chinese to Modern Chinese task the first step of data post-processing is to remove space and the second step is to restore simplified Chinese characters to traditional Chinese characters to satisfy the submission requirements. In the Ancient Chinese to English task the first step of data post-processing is to remove extra space.Secondly we restore the case of the English results.

3. Experiments

The aims of experiment are to verify (1) whether context awareness models can provide more information gain; (2) which one of the inside-context and outside-context model performs

---

[6] Ganaie M A, Hu M, Malik A K, et al. Ensemble deep learning: A review[J]. Engineering Applications of Artificial Intelligence, 2022, 115: 105151.

better; (3) which one of the source laguage context and Pinyin coding contexts performs better. We use BLEU4[7] to evaluate the quality of the translations, which is automatic evaluation index of machine translation commonly used now.

3.1. System Settings

We trained our machine translation model by the Fairseq sequence modeling toolkit of PyTorch. The main parameters are set as follows: each model uses 1-3 GPUs, batch size is 2048, parameter update frequency is 1, learning rate is 5e-4, and the number of warmup steps is 4000. Maximum number of tokens is 4096. Self-attention mechanism uses 16 heads.The dropout is 0.3. BPE is 32K.Loss function is label smoothed cross entropy.Adam betas is (0.9,0.997). Maximum epoch is 40. Initial learning rate is 0.0005,Context-aware learning rate is 0.0001.

3.2. Data Preprocessing

The data include the released parallel data and external data of monolingual languages. For the Ancient-Chinese-to-English machine translation task we use the released data and Twenty-four Histories (ancient Chinese monolingual data). For the Ancient-Chinese-to-English machine translation task, we adopte the released data and Zizhi Tongjian (ancient Chinese monolingual data). Forward translation generates the pseudo-parallel[8] corpus as supplementary data. Both forward translation and the released data are preprocessed to reduce data noise:
1. Duplicating;
2. Traditional Chinese to Simplified Chinese: zhconv[9] is used to convert;
3. Full-width characters to half-width characters: Niutrans[10] preprocessing toolkit;
4.Tokenization: urheen[11] for modern Chinese and jiayan[12] package for ancient Chinese;
5. Sentence length ratio filtering: we retain sentences with length ratio in [0.1,10];
6. Pinyin coding: xpinyin[13] is used to generate Pinyin for source sentences;

The number of sentences with preprocessing results is listed in Table 1. The partition of sentence is shown in Table 2.

Table 1. The statistics of preprocessed data.

Type	Before preprocessing	After preprocessing

[7] Papineni K, Roukos S, Ward T, et al. Bleu: a method for automatic evaluation of machine translation[C]//Proceedings of the 40th annual meeting of the Association for Computational Linguistics. 2002: 311-318.
[8] Haddow B, Bawden R, Barone A V M, et al. Survey of low-resource machine translation[J]. Computational Linguistics, 2022, 48(3): 673-732
[9] nobodxbodon.zhconverter.https://github.com/nobodxbodon/zhconverter
[10] NiuTrans. NiuTrans: An Open Source Neural Machine Translation Toolkit. https://github.com/NiuTrans/NiuTrans.
[11] Chinese Academy of Sciences, Institute of Automation. Chinese Information Processing Software Download. https://www.nlpr.ia.ac.cn/cip/software.html.
[12] Jiayan. Jiayan: Chinese word segmentation in Python.https://github.com/jiaeyan/Jiayan.
[13] lxneng. Xpinyin: Convert chinese hanzi to pinyin.https://github.com/lxneng/xpinyin.

	(Sentence pair)	(Sentence pair)
Released bilingual data in a2m	307,494	303,164
Zizhi Tongjian data	319,883	312,389
Released bilingual data in a2e	5,899	5,898
Twenty-four Histories data	305,163	305,162

Table 2. The partition of data

Task	train	dev	test
a2m	553,998	30,777	30,777
a2e	279,954	15,553	15,53

3.3. Baseline systems

We use three Transformer model architectures as baseline systems in this evaluation:
(1) Transformer: It is based on the Transformer architecture, which is suitable for handling medium-sized translation tasks. Compared with the larger model, it requires less training data and computational resources, but may be inferior in performance.
(2) Transformer_wmt_en_de_big: It is suitable for multilingual translation tasks.
(3) Transformer_wmt_en_de_big_t2t: It is an end-to-end machine learning framework with the Tensor2Tensor (T2T) framework for training.

3.4. Experimental Results

3.4.1. Context Performance

Tables 3-4 show the results of baseline model and context-awareness-based model for Ancient Chinese to Modern Chinese task and Ancient Chinese to English task. In baseline model 1-3, we only use the released bilingual corpus while in baseline model 4 we use both released corpus and pseudo-bilingual data.The difference between baseline models is model architectures. Baseline model 1-3 are transformer, transformer_wmt_en_de_big, and transformer_wmt_en_de_big_t2t. And the baseline model 4 use the same architectures as baseline model 3. Inside-context system means the inside-context awareness model. Outside-context system represents the outside context-awareness model, Gaussian context means gaussian noise as context. Src means source language sentence as context, Src.Pinyin coding means the Pinyin coding of source language as context.

Table 3. Performance comparison of a2m
(Baseline1-3 only use released data, other models use whole data)

System	BLEU (%)
Baseline 1(arch = transformer)	37.35
Baseline 2(arch = transformer_wmt_en_de_big)	37.80
Baseline 3(arch = transformer_wmt_en_de_big_t2t)	38.03
Baseline 4(transformer_wmt_en_de_big_t2t+ pseudo-bilingual)	38.15
Transformer(Src)	38.57
Inside-context(Src)	38.97
Outisde-context(Src)	39.26
Transformer(Src.Pinyin coding)	37.81

Inside-context(Src.Pinyin coding)	38.98
Outisde-context(Src.Pinyin coding)	38.92
Gaussian-context(Src.Pinyin coding)	39.00

From Table 3 the most effective model among baseline 1-4, is the baseline 4 which is based on Transformer_wmt_en_de_big_t2t plus pseudo-bilingual data and achieves a BLEU score of 38.15, improving up to 0.8% BLEU compare with baseline 1. By comparing the Transformer(Src) with Basline 4 ,we found just generating bpe dict with context information also helps a little though the constructure of modesl is not changed. Among context-awareness model of source language as contexts, the outside-context performs the better with a BLEU score of 39.26. When Pinyin coding is used as contexts, the inside-context performs best with a BLEU score of 38.98.

Table 4. Performance comparison of a2e
(Baseline1-3 only use released data, other models use whole data)

System	BLEU (%)
Baseline 1(arch = transformer)	4.19
Baseline 2(arch = transformer_wmt_en_de_big)	5.32
Baseline 3(arch = transformer_wmt_en_de_big_t2t)	6.09
Baseline 4(arch=transformer_wmt_en_de_big_t2t+ pseudo-bilingual)	17.44
Transformer(Src)	18.16
Inside-context(Src)	18.38
Outisde-context(Src)	18.18
Transformer(Src.Pinyin coding)	17.49
Inside-context(Src.Pinyin coding)	18.48
Outisde-context(Src.Pinyin coding)	18.46
Gaussian-context(Src.Pinyin coding)	18.51

From Table 4 data enhancement also effectively improves translation performance. Transformer_wmt_en_de_big_t2t + pseudo-bilingual data achieves a BLEU score of 17.44, improving up to 13.25% BLEU compare with baseline 1. And in both type of contexts, inside-context preforms better But the Gaussian performs best.

3.4.2. Ensemble Performance

Table 5-6 compare the result of context-awareness-based model with ensemble. The strategy is seperately combined with inside-context model and gaussian model. The ensemble approach did not perform well both in a2m and a2e. After the ensemble our model BLEU score dropped by 0.3%.

Table 5. Comparison of context-awareness model for a2m

System	BLEU (Src)	BLEU (Src.Pinyin coding)
Inside-context+ensemble	38.58	38.62

Gaussian-context+ensem-ble	38.85

Table 6. Comparison of context-awareness model for a2e

System	BLE（Src）	BLEU（Src.Pinyin coding）
Inside-context+ensemble	18.14	18.12
Gaussian-context+ensemble	18.51	

We submitted the result of Gaussian-context+ensemble for Ancient Chinese to Modern Chinese task and the result of Gaussian-context+ensemble for Ancient Chinese to English tasks.

4. Conclusion

This paper presents the main methods of ISTIC's Machine Translation System in Eva-Han(2023). Our model is based on the Transformer architecture and context-awareness model. We used Forward translation to enhance the training data. This strategy works well when data is scarce such as in a2e task, and has a little boost when data is more sufficient, such as in a2m task.The context-awareness methods can effectively improve the translation performance whether the contexts are source language or source language's Pinyin coding. But the ensemble did not work very well.

For future work, there are many interesting directions. Firstly we will study how to mine the linguistic knowledge between ancient Chinese and modern Chinese and integrate it into the context informtion. Secondly we will continue to improve the contexts-awareness based model both on encoder layer and decoder layer.

References

Bei Li, Hui Liu, Ziyang Wang, Yufan Jiang, Tong Xiao, Jingbo Zhu, Tongran Liu, and Chang-liang Li. 2020. Does Multi-Encoder Help? A Case Study on Context-Aware Neural Machine Translation. In Proceedings of the 58th Annual Meeting of the Association for Computational Linguistics, pages 3512 – 3518, Online. Association for Computational Linguistics.

Chinese Academy of Sciences, Institute of Automation. Chinese Information Processing Software Download. https://www.nlpr.ia.ac.cn/cip/software.html.

Facebook Research. Fairseq: A Fast, Extensible Toolkit for Sequence Modeling. Github, 2016, https://github.com/facebookresearch/fairseq.

Fernandes, P., Yin, K., Neubig, G., & Martins, A. F. T. (2018). Measuring and Increasing Con -text Usage in Context-Aware Machine Translation. In Proceedings of the 2018 Conference of the North American Chapter of the Association for Computational Linguistics: Huma Language Technologies, Volume 1 (Long Papers) (pp. 1114-1123).

Ganaie M A, Hu M, Malik A K, et al. Ensemble deep learning: A review[J]. Engineering Appl ications of Artificial Intelligence, 2022, 115: 105151.

Haddow B, Bawden R, Barone A V M, et al. Survey of low-resource machine translation[J]. C omputational Linguistics, 2022, 48(3): 673-732

lxneng. Xpinyin: Convert chinese hanzi to pinyin.https://github.com/lxneng/xpinyin.

Jiayan. Jiayan: Chinese word segmentation in Python.https://github.com/jiaeyan/Jiayan.

Nishant Kambhatla, Logan Born, and Anoop Sarkar. 2022. CipherDAug: Ciphertext based Data Augmentation for Neural Machine Translation. In Proceedings of the 60th Annual Meeting of the Association for Computational Linguistics (Volume 1: Long Papers), pages 201 – 21 8, Dublin, Ireland. Association for Computational Linguistics.

NiuTrans. NiuTrans: An Open Source Neural Machine Translation Toolkit.https://github.com/Niu Trans/NiuTrans.

Nobodxbodon.zhconverter.https://github.com/nobodxbodon/zhconverter

Papineni K, Roukos S, Ward T, et al. Bleu: a method for automatic evaluation of machine tran slation[C]//Proceedings of the 40th annual meeting of the Association for Computational Li nguistics. 2002: 311-318.

Vaswani, A., et al.: Attention is all you need. In: Advances in Neural Information Processing Systems 30 (NIPS 2017), pp. 5998–6008 (2017)

BIT-ACT: An Ancient Chinese Translation System Using Data Augmentation

Li Zeng zengli@bit.edu.cn
Beijing Institute of Technology, Beijing, 100081, China
Yanzhi Tian tianyanzhi@bit.edu.cn
Beijing Institute of Technology, Beijing, 100081, China
Yingyu Shan shanyingyu@bit.edu.cn
Beijing Institute of Technology, Beijing, 100081, China
Yuhang Guo* guoyuhang@bit.edu.cn
Beijing Institute of Technology, Beijing, 100081, China

Abstract

This paper describes a translation model for ancient Chinese to modern Chinese and English for the Evahan 2023 competition, a subtask of the Ancient Language Translation 2023 challenge. During the training of our model, we applied various data augmentation techniques and used SiKu-RoBERTa as part of our model architecture. The results indicate that back translation improves the model's performance, but double back translation introduces noise and harms the model's performance. Fine-tuning on the original dataset can be helpful in solving the issue.

1 Introduction

Ancient Chinese translation is a Machine Translation task, aiming to translate ancient Chinese into modern Chinese or English, which is of great significance for the research and understanding of ancient Chinese. In the area of ancient Chinese translation, the presence of unique features in ancient Chinese poses challenges. Ancient Chinese has its own distinctive features, including a large number of rare characters, characters with different meanings in ancient and modern times. In the aspect of syntax, ancient Chinese are very different from modern Chinese, including lots of inverted or elliptical sentences, which increases the difficulty in translation. Maksym and Tetyana (2015) Additionally, due to the limited amount of data, it's necessary to apply data augmentation during training.

In our system, we use a transformer (Vaswani et al., 2017) architecture with adjusted parameters, to address the limited data, we applied various data augmentation techniques to generate additional data, achieved improved performance. Considering the unique grammatical structures of ancient Chinese, we tried a BERT Devlin et al. (2018) model pre-trained on ancient Chinese, we had analyzed different results from these approaches.

*Corresponding Author

Proceedings of ALT2023: First Workshop on Ancient Language Translation, pages 43–47
September 5, 2023, Macau SAR, China.

2 Method

In this section, we introduce our data processing and augmentation method. We also describe the architecture of our systems.

2.1 Data Processing

Training data for evaluation is excerpted from the Twenty-Four Histories(dynastic histories from remote antiquity till the Ming Dynasty), the Pre-Qin classics and "ZiZhi TongJian (Comprehensive Mirror in Aid of Governance)". The Twenty-Four Histories is the general name for the 24 official histories written by the various dynasties in ancient China. The Pre-Qin classics refer to historical materials from the Pre-Qin period (Paleolithic Period 221 B.C.), which play an important role in ancient books, including history books and subsidiary texts. "Zizhi Tongjian" is a multi-volume chronological history book compiled by Sima Guang, a historian of the Northern Song Dynasty. It covers 1,362 years of history of the sixteen dynasties.The Chinese ancient classic texts in the corpus exhibit diachronicity, spanning thousands of years and encompassing the four traditional types of Chinese canonical texts: Jing (Classics), Shi (Histories), Zi (Philosophical Works), and Ji (Literary Works)."

We conduct the following data processing method:

1. Because of the lack of segmentation for datasets, we apply segmentation with 'jieba' [1].

2. Apply 15K BPE (Byte-Pair-Encoding) (Sennrich et al., 2016) to the datasets.

3. Discard extremely long sentences (2048 tokens without BERT and 512 tokens with BERT) during training.

4. Randomly select validation sets: extract 2000 sentences from the Twenty-Four Histories and 40 sentences from Zizhi Tongjian.

After data processing, the quantities of the data are as follows:

Dataset	Sentences	Tokens
Ancient Chinese train set	311,352	7,912,087
Modern Chinese train set	311,352	9,495,032
Ancient Chinese valid set	2,040	51,875
Modern Chinese valid set	2,040	62,626

Table 1: Statistic of Datasets

2.2 Data Augmentation

Due to the limited size of the dataset and the constraints imposed by the closed track, where the use of external data is restricted, we employed various data augmentation techniques to augment the available data and enhance the capability of our model.

To apply data augmentation, we trained models for modern Chinese to ancient Chinese translation .Using these models, we translated the training set data, obtained new data in ancient Chinese, then mixed it with the original data, Then retrain a new model with mixed data. Which is commonly referred to as back translated(BT)Edunov et al. (2018). Notice that the vocabulary of the data may have changed after each back translation, we had apply BPE and preprocess on training data again. Details will be provided in selection 3.

[1] `https://github.com/fxsjy/jieba`

2.3 Model

We employed the transformer model provided by fairseq [2] Ott et al. (2019) as our architecture, based on the scale of the dataset, we conducted experiments using the following parameters.

Parameter	Value
Attention Heads	4
Number of Layers	6
Embedding Dimension	512
Feed-forward Hidden Size	1024

Table 2: Model Hyperparameters

Due to the limited amount of data, we also explored the use of pre-trained models. In our research, we employed SiKu-RoBERTa [3]Wang et al. (2022) as a pre-trained model. SiKu-RoBERTa is based on the RoBERTa model architecture and was trained on the complete text corpus of the "Si Ku Quan Shu" , a large-scale series of books compiled during the Qianlong period of the Qing Dynasty. We believe that SiKu-RoBERTa has the ability to capture rich knowledge of the ancient Chinese language.

3 Experiments

In this section, we delve into the training details and steps, including the utilization of hyperparameters. We also compare and analyze the results obtained from different models.

For the Model Configuration, we used the following set of Model Configuration as the default. We will point out if there are any modifications. We usd Adam Kingma and Ba (2014) as our optimizer, use the "inverse sqrt lr" scheduler with 4000 warm-up steps.

Configuration	Value
optimizer	Adam
lr-scheduler	inverse_sqrt
learning-rate	0.00005
dropout	0.2
weight-decay	0.0001

Table 3: Model Configuration

We conducted the training on two TITAN X GPUs, for each model, we trained for a total of 300,000 updates.

3.1 Ancient Chinese-Modern Chinese

In the task of translating ancient Chinese to modern Chinese, we experimented with a range of data augmentation strategies and evaluated the effectiveness of the RoBERTa model. Through extensive testing, we assessed the performance of these models and identified several factors that could lead to results.

First, we trained a baseline model using the given dataset and the configuration above.

[2]https://github.com/facebookresearch/fairseq

[3]https://github.com/hsc748NLP/SikuBERT-for-digital-humanities-and-classical-Chinese-information-processing

Then, we utilized the aforementioned data augmentation technique and trained a model for modern Chinese to ancient Chinese translation. Using this model, we performed one round of back-translation (BT) on the original dataset.

After retraining the model using the data augmented through back translation, we obtained a new model. We observed a significant improvement in the model's performance after the back translation process. Encouraged by these results, we performed the same back translation operation once again, to examine whether further improvement can be achieved. It was referred to as double back translation (double BT)

However, in reality, the double back translation didn't achieve the expected results. We suspect that this might due to the introduction of additional noise in the generated data. Considering this, we revert back to the original data, and fine-tune out model using the original dataset.

Finally, we tried to incorporate the BERT model. We used SiKu-RoBERTa as the embedding layer for the encoder.Zhu et al. (2020) After each training method, we evaluated the model's performance on valid set using the BLEU Papineni et al. (2002) score. The results are as follows.

Model	BLEU
baseline	32.4
BT	36.4
double-BT	35.2
double-BT and fine-tune	36.9
SiKu-RoBERTa	29.8

Table 4: BLEU Score of Ancient Chinese-Modern Chinese Model

3.2 Ancient Chinese-English

Considering the provided parallel text is limited, directly train the model on original text may not yield satisfactory results. Therefore, we only tested the method of training the model on the generated data.

First, we trained a baseline model using the provided ancient Chinese to English test. Due to data is limited, we were using dropout=0.4 Srivastava et al. (2014) to avoid overfitting.

Then, we generated data by decoding ancient Chinese in "Twenty-Four Histories"

Finally, we trained a new model using only the newly generated data. This model is served as our final model for the ancient Chinese to English translation task.

3.3 Official Evaluation Results

We used the best-performing model mentioned above to translate the official provided data and submitted it for testing. The results are as follows:

Translation Direction	BLEU
Ancient Chinese - Modern Chinese	21.95
Ancient Chinese - English	1.11

Table 5: Officially Evaluated BLEU Scores

The BLEU score obtained after submission showed a significant deviation from the scores we observed during local testing. We believe this discrepancy might be attributed to the model overfitting to a certain extent or due to poor performance on the specific corpus likely caused by differences in the source of the data.

4 Conclusion

For the ancient Chinese to modern Chinese task, we found that back translation can help improve the model's performance with limited data. However, it's important to notice that back translation may introduce noise, and fine-tuning the model after back translation could potentially enhance its performance.

When using RoBERTa as embedding, the results were not as expected. One possible reason is that we did not train RoBERTa model on our data separately, leading to mismatch in vocabulary. Additionally, the large scale of RoBERTa might cause overfitting, We believe that more data will help address this issue.

For the ancient Chinese to English task, due to the limited dataset and significant linguistic differences between ancient Chinese and Endlish, we did not achieve satisfactory results.

References

Devlin, J., Chang, M.-W., Lee, K., and Toutanova, K. (2018). Bert: Pre-training of deep bidirectional transformers for language understanding. *arXiv preprint arXiv:1810.04805*.

Edunov, S., Ott, M., Auli, M., and Grangier, D. (2018). Understanding back-translation at scale. *arXiv preprint arXiv:1808.09381*.

Kingma, D. P. and Ba, J. (2014). Adam: A method for stochastic optimization. *arXiv preprint arXiv:1412.6980*.

Maksym, K. and Tetyana, S. (2015). Lexical difficulties in translation of ancient chinese texts into the ukrainian and english languages (case study of the chinese treatise "the art of war" and its translations into the ukrainian and english languages). *SECTION II. CROSS-CULTURAL COMMUNICATION IN CONTEMPORARY GEOPOLITICAL SPACE*, page 24.

Ott, M., Edunov, S., Baevski, A., Fan, A., Gross, S., Ng, N., Grangier, D., and Auli, M. (2019). fairseq: A fast, extensible toolkit for sequence modeling. In *Proceedings of NAACL-HLT 2019: Demonstrations*.

Papineni, K., Roukos, S., Ward, T., and Zhu, W.-J. (2002). Bleu: a method for automatic evaluation of machine translation. In *Proceedings of the 40th annual meeting of the Association for Computational Linguistics*, pages 311–318.

Sennrich, R., Haddow, B., and Birch, A. (2016). Neural machine translation of rare words with subword units.

Srivastava, N., Hinton, G., Krizhevsky, A., Sutskever, I., and Salakhutdinov, R. (2014). Dropout: a simple way to prevent neural networks from overfitting. *The journal of machine learning research*, 15(1):1929–1958.

Vaswani, A., Shazeer, N., Parmar, N., Uszkoreit, J., Jones, L., Gomez, A. N., Kaiser, L. u., and Polosukhin, I. (2017). Attention is all you need. In Guyon, I., Luxburg, U. V., Bengio, S., Wallach, H., Fergus, R., Vishwanathan, S., and Garnett, R., editors, *Advances in Neural Information Processing Systems*, volume 30. Curran Associates, Inc.

Wang, D., Liu, C., Zhu, Z., Feng, J., Hu, H., Shen, S., and Li, B. (2022). Construction and application of pre-training model of "siku quanshu" oriented to digital humanities. *Library Tribune*, 42(6):31–43.

Zhu, J., Xia, Y., Wu, L., He, D., Qin, T., Zhou, W., Li, H., and Liu, T.-Y. (2020). Incorporating bert into neural machine translation. *arXiv preprint arXiv:2002.06823*.

Technical Report on Ancient Chinese Machine Translation Based on mRASP Model

Wenjing Liu 18851091773@163.com

Jing Xie* Xie_Hugh@njucm.edu.cn

School of Health Economics and Management, Nanjing University of Chinese Medicine, Nanjing, 210046, China

Abstract: Objective This paper aims to improve the performance of machine translation of ancient Chinese classics, which can better promote the development of ancient books research and the spread of Chinese culture. **Methods** Based on the multilingual translation machine pre-training model of mRASP, the model was trained by fine-tuning the specific language pairs, namely a2m, and a2e, according to the two downstream tasks of classical Chinese translation into modern Chinese and classical Chinese translation into English, using the parallel corpus of ancient white and white and ancient English parallel corpus of Pre-Qin+ZiZhiTongJian, and the translation performance of the fine-tuning model was evaluated by BIEU evaluation index. **Results** The BIEU4 results of the three downstream tasks of 24_histories_a2m、Pre-Qin+ZiZhiTongJian_a2m、 Pre-Qin+ZiZhiTongJian_a2e were 17.38, 13.69 and 12.90 respectively.

1 Introduction

Ancient Chinese classics are an important part of Chinese traditional culture. How to mention the automatic translation effect of ancient books is an important topic in the study of ancient Chinese classics. Improving machine translation performance from ancient Chinese to modern Chinese can better promote the development of ancient book research. At the same time, improving the machine translation technology from ancient Chinese to English can also promote the promotion of Chinese traditional culture in the world. EvaHan 2023 is the second international evaluation of ancient Chinese information processing. This evaluation task is the machine translation of ancient Chinese, including two sub-tasks: translating ancient Chinese into modern Chinese; ancient Chinese into English.

*Corresponding author: Jing Xie Ph.D., Associate Professor, School of Health Economics and Management, Nanjing University of Chinese Medicine. Main research directions : natural language processing, intelligence analysis and evaluation based on information technology

Proceedings of ALT2023: First Workshop on Ancient Language Translation, pages 48–54
September 5, 2023, Macau SAR, China.

This evaluation is divided into two modes: open mode and closed mode. The team chooses the open mode and selects the multi-language translation pre-training model-mRASP released by ByteDance in 2020. Based on this pre-training model, the specific language pairs are fine-tuned, that is, a2c and a2e, to realize the translation of classical Chinese into modern Chinese and English.

2 Multilingual translation model mRASP

2.1 The design motivation of mRASP

mRASP is a recent multilingual translation byte-beating AI Lab at EMNLP2020-Multilingual Random Aligned Substitution Pre-training (mRASP) (Lin et al, 2019). It aims to implement BERT in the field of machine translation and proposes a universal machine translation model. At present, it has become a new successful paradigm of NLP to pre-train the model with a large amount of easily available data and to fine-tune the model with a small amount of labeled data in specific application scenarios to achieve the model available in actual scenarios. For example, after pre-training on large-scale plain text, BERT (Devlin et al, 2018) can achieve good results with a small amount of fine-tuning on multiple natural language processing tasks. However, in multilingual machine translation, the paradigm of pre-training and fine-tuning has not yet achieved universal success. The previous NLP pre-training methods such as BERT and GPT(Radford et al, 2018) have a large gap between the training objectives and the translation focus and are not easy to use directly. MRASP proposes a new idea, which uses a large number of bilingual parallel corpora that have been accumulated in multiple languages to combine and train a unified model, and then fine-tune based on this, so that the pre-training and fine-tuning objectives are as close as possible, to give full play to the role of the pre-training model.

For machine translation, the translation ability is transferred to different languages, so that the information between different languages can be used to each other, thus mentioning the effect of machine translation. Based on this consideration, the design method of mRASP is to design a general pre-training model to learn the commonality of conversion between languages, and then it is easier to migrate to a new translation direction. The design of mRASP follows two basic principles: first, the goal of pre-training is the same as that of machine translation, and it is necessary to learn the language conversion ability; second, learn the universal representation of language as much as possible. For cross-language sentences or words, if the semantics are close, the representation in the hidden space should also be close.

2.2 mRASP model framework

The mRASP follows a common pre-training-fine-tuning framework. In the pre-training stage, mRASP uses multi-lingual parallel data as the main goal of pre-training. The data sets of 32 open language pairs are put into the same model for joint training and then fine-tuned according to the specific language pairs. The neural network structure uses Transformer, plus a language token to identify the source language and the target language. To ensure that sentences and words of different languages can be embedded into the same space, sentences with the same meaning should be corresponding to the same vector representation in both Chinese and English, and the random substitution alignment technique RAS is introduced to create richer context, It makes the words with similar meanings in different languages closer in the vector space. This method can connect the semantic space between different languages, which greatly improves the final translation effect.

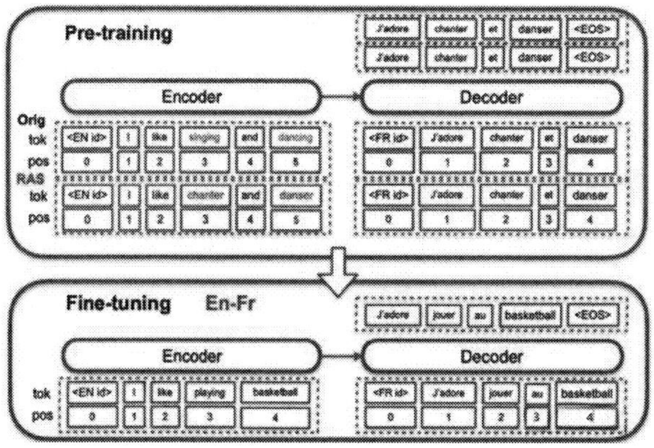

Figure 1 mRASP pre-training model framework

2.3 The role of the mRASP model

The mRASP model confirms for the first time that the multilingual machine translation model can be applied to improve the machine translation model with rich corpus resources. For the first time, the concept of ' zero-shot translation ' in multilingual neural machine translation is extended to 'exotic translation' and divided into four scenarios. In addition, mRASP can even improve the translation quality of exotic languages which has never appeared in the pre-training corpus. The four scenarios of mRASP extended 'exotic translation ' are as follows:

Exotic Pair: Although both the source language and the target language have been pre-trained, they are separated in the pre-training stage ;

Exotic Source: The source language is not pre-trained, and the target language is pre-trained ;

Exotic Target: The source language is pre-trained, and the target language is not pre-trained ;

Exotic Full: Neither the source language nor the target language was pre-trained.

3 Downstream language pair fine-tuning experiment based on mRASP model

3.1 Source of corpus

This experiment uses the data provided by the second international evaluation of automatic analysis of ancient Chinese EvaHan (Ancient Chinese Machine Translation), including the ancient and white parallel corpus of China's twenty-four histories, the pre-Qin classics, and the ancient and English parallel corpus of 'Zi Zhi Tong Jian'.All the corpora in the experiment are divided into training sets and verification sets according to the ratio of 9:1.The specific expected basic data statistics are shown in Table 1.

Table 1 Basic data statistics of the training corpus

Data set	The number of ancient characters	Number of characters in translation
24_history ancient white parallel corpus	9,583,749words	12,763,534words
Pre-Qin classics and 'Zizhi Tongjian' ancient English parallel corpus	618,083words	838,321words

3.2 Data preprocessing

Data preprocessing for the corpus is an important part of machine translation. The quality of corpus processing determines the effect of the machine translation system training model to a certain extent. According to the data requirements of the mRASP model, the training set and the validation set are preprocessed at the same time. The main preprocessing steps are as follows:1)Data filtering and cleaning;2) The joint BPE sub-vocabulary is used for word segmentation;3)Binarize the data using the fairseq-preparing command.

3.3 Experimental model parameters and evaluation index

In this paper, Transformer is used as the baseline model, which consists of 6 encoder layers and 6 decoder layers. The hyperparameters of the training model in this experiment are shown in Table 2.

Table 2 The main super parameter settings of the experiment

Super parameter	value
batch_size	512
Learn rating	0.0001
label_smoothing	0.1
dropout	0.3
Update frequency	10
warmup_init_lr	1e-07
fp16	True

In this experiment, BIEU, a commonly used indicator,was used to evaluate the performance of the fine-tuned pre-trained model.BLEU (Bilingual Evaluation Understudy), an automatic evaluation method proposed by IBM researchers in 2002, is currently the most widely used automatic evaluation index (Papineni et al, 2002), by using n-gram matching to evaluate the similarity between the machine translation result and the reference answer, the closer the machine translation is to the reference answer, the higher its quality is determined. The larger the n value is, the larger the matching fragment considered in the evaluation is. The calculation of BLEU first considers the matching rate of the n-gram in the reference answer in the machine translation to be evaluated, which is called n-gram Precision. The calculation method is as follows :

$$P_n = \frac{count_{hit}}{count_{output}}$$

Among them， $count_{hit}$ indicates the number of n-gram hits in the machine translation in the reference answer， $count_{output}$ denotes the total number of n-grams in machine translation. To avoid the same word being repeated calculation, The definition of BLEU is defined by truncation $count_{hit}$ and $count_{output}$.

3.4 Experimental results

Based on the mRASP model, the experiment of translating classical Chinese into modern Chinese and classical Chinese into English is carried out. The research data set is based on the whole sentence. The specific experimental results are shown in Table 3.

Table 3 Experimental evaluation results

Machine Translation Tasks	BIEU-4
24_histories_a2m	17.38
Pre-Qin+ZiZhiTongJian_a2m	13.69
Pre-Qin+ZiZhiTongJian_a2e	12.90

4 Conclusion

This group uses the mRASP multi-language translation machine pre-training model and fine-tunes the specific language pairs of the model according to the two downstream tasks of classical Chinese translation into modern Chinese and classical Chinese translation into English. Firstly, the parallel corpus of specific language pairs is cleaned, segmented, and binarized. Secondly, the generated data is fine-tuned on the mRASP pre-training model, and the translation performance of the fine-tuned model is evaluated by the BIEU evaluation index. Since the source language classical Chinese is not pre-trained in mRASP, while modern and English are trained as target languages, the model training of this language pair belongs to the scenario of 'Exotic Source', and the BIEU value obtained is small. In future work, we can continue to use the mRASP2 (Pan et al, 2021) pre-training model for fine-tuning training. mRASP2 combines 32 language datasets and generates a total of 64 directional translation pairs. On the Transformer model of multilingual translation, a comparative learning task is added at the top of the encoder (Encoder) end to further improve the translation performance.

References:

Zehui Lin, Xiao Pan, Mingxuan Wang, Xipeng Qiu, Jiangtao Feng, Hao Zhou, and Lei Li,J,(2019).Pre-training Multilingual Neural Machine Translation by Leveraging Alignment Information. DOI: https://doi.org/10.48550/arXiv.2010.03142

Jacob Devlin, Ming-Wei Chang, Kenton Lee, and Kristina Toutanova, J. (2018). BERT: Pre-training of Deep Bidirectional Transformers for Language Understanding.

Radford, A., Narasimhan, K., Salimans, T., & Sutskever, I. (2018). Improving language understanding by generative pre-training.

Kishore Papineni, Salim Roukos, Todd Ward, and Wei-Jing Zhu. 2002. Bleu: a Method for Automatic Evaluation of Machine Translation. In Proceedings of the 40th Annual Meeting of the Association for Computational Linguistics, pages 311–318, Philadelphia, Pennsylvania, USA. Association for Computational Linguistics.

Xiao Pan, Mingxuan Wang, Liwei Wu, and Lei Li, J. (2021). Contrastive Learning for Many-to-many Multilingual Neural Machine Translation.arXiv:2105.09501

AnchiLm: An Effective Classical-to-Modern Chinese Translation Model Leveraging bpe-drop and SikuRoBERTa

Jiahui Zhu miugod0126@gmail.com
School of Optical-Electrical and Computer Engineering, University of Shanghai for Science and Technology, Shanghai, 200093, China

Sizhou Chen jjyaoao@126.com
Blockchain Industry College, Chengdu University of Information Technology, Chengdu, 610225, China

Abstract

In this paper, we present our submitted model for translating ancient to modern texts, which ranked sixth in the closed track of ancient Chinese in the 2nd International Review of Automatic Analysis of Ancient Chinese (EvaHan). Specifically, we employed two strategies to improve the translation from ancient to modern texts. First, we used bpe-drop to enhance the parallel corpus. Second, we use SikuRoBERTa to simultaneously initialize the translation model's codec and reconstruct the bpe word list. In our experiments, we compare the baseline model, rdrop, pre-trained model, and parameter initialization methods. The experimental results show that the parameter initialization method in this paper significantly outperforms the baseline model in terms of performance, and its BLEU score reaches **21.75**.

1 Introduction

Ancient Chinese historical texts are not only key parts of Chinese civilization but treasures of global culture. Understanding these works is challenging for modern people, hence, translation is vital to bridge this gap. Traditional manual translation of these texts is time-consuming and challenging. With the advancement of computer science, Machine Translation (MT) provides a new solution to this problem. Among various MT methods, Neural Machine Translation (NMT) is representative.

However, applying NMT to ancient text translation faces significant challenges. The main issue is the relatively small corpus for ancient text translation, making it hard for models to learn and capture the complex grammar and rich semantics from limited data. Further, as shown in **Figure 1**, the conversion between modern and ancient Chinese is highly complicated. Consequently, the results of ancient text translation often fall short of expectations.

In recent years, the "pre-training + fine-tuning" paradigm has become a powerful technique in the field of Neural Machine Translation (NMT). Researchers have attempted to leverage this paradigm to enhance translation models, such as XLM Conneau and Lample (2019) , MASS-Song et al. (2019) , mBARTLiu et al. (2020) , and mRASP2Pan et al. (2021) , which have performed excellently in machine translation tasks. Meanwhile, there have also been some excellent solutions in the field of ancient text translation. For instance, a Transformer model was

Proceedings of ALT2023: First Workshop on Ancient Language Translation, pages 55–60
September 5, 2023, Macau SAR, China.

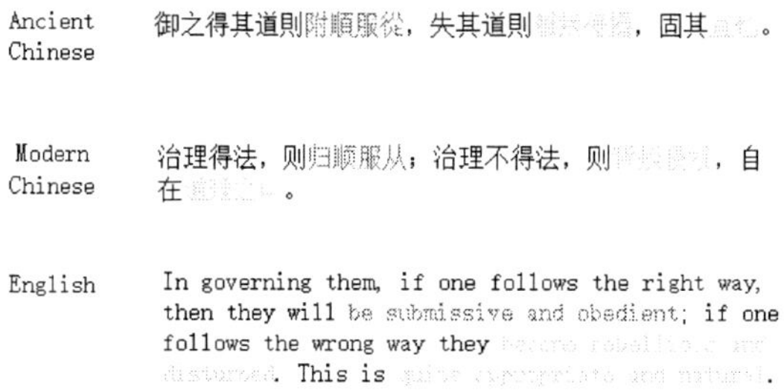

Figure 1: Changes in Linguistic Features between Modern Chinese and Ancient Chinese

trained to translate ancient Chinese into modern Chinese , AnchiBERTLiu et al. (2019) pre-trained BERTDevlin et al. (2018) on ancient texts and then initialized the encoder of the NMT model, or the Bert-FusedZhu et al. (2020) method fused the BERT output into every layer of the encoder-decoder using the attention mechanism...

Existing research provides a series of valuable insights. In this paper, we aim to further advance research in this field by proposing **AnchiLM** to deal with specific problems and challenges more effectively. It has the following main features:

1) We initialize the encoder with the SikuRoberta model pre-trained on the Siku Quanshu, and introduce the method of alternating initialization from Deltalm[9] to initialize the decoder parameters.

2) We noticed that when using the SikuRoberta model, tokenizing at the character level could lead to excessively long translation sequences. To address this issue, we encode sentences in a mixed character-word manner and initialize the new vocabulary embedding with the topn character embedding vectors.

3) We introduce bpe-drop, a simple and effective subword regularization method. It randomly disrupts the BPE segmentation process, resulting in multiple segmentations within the same fixed BPE framework.

2 Methods

In this section, we will detail the methodology of our approach, which consists of three main components: the encoder, the decoder, and the word embedding. Each of these components plays a crucial role in our translation model.

2.1 Encoder

Based on the idea of domain adaptation training, SikuRoBERTa continues to train on the basis of the RoBERTa structure combined with a large amount of ancient Chinese corpus from "Siku Quanshu", so as to obtain a pre-training model for the ancient Chinese field. It can provide rich semantic information of ancient texts. We take SikuRoBERTa to initialize the encoder parameters.

2.2 Decoder

Since the Transformer decoder adds a cross-attention layer to each layer of Bert to capture the correlation between the source language and the target language, this paper uses the alternate initialization method proposed in deltalm to self-attention in each layer of the decoder. A feed-forward layer is inserted in the middle of cross-attention, so that the two layers of bert initialize one layer of the decoder, thus fully initializing the six-layer decoder.

2.3 Word Embedding

In response to the problem that the word-level tokenization of Chinese SikuRoBERTa leads to excessively long sentences, low encoding efficiency, and difficulty in training convergence, this paper rebuilds the vocabulary at the subword level. Specifically, the ancient text and modern text are merged and jointly trained with BPE to build a unified vocabulary. Then for each token in the new vocabulary, the SikuRoBERTa word embedding vector of its first character is taken to initialize the vocabulary.

In summary, our approach combines a pre-trained encoder, a specially initialized decoder, and a reconstructed vocabulary to effectively handle the challenges of ancient text translation. The detailed structure of our model is illustrated in **Figure 2**.

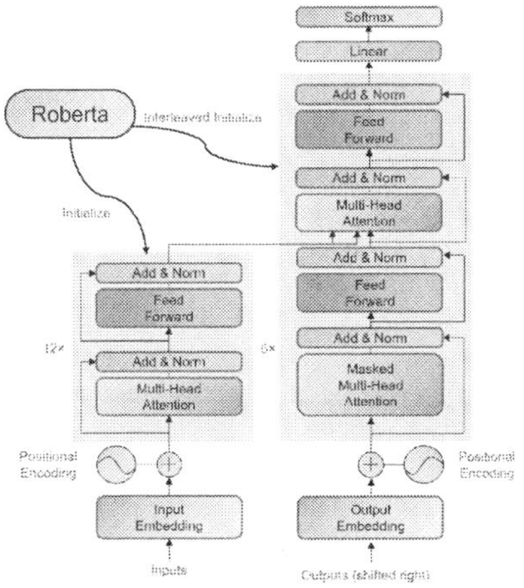

Figure 2: AnchiLm model structure diagram

3 Experiment

For the introduction of the experimental data, we put it in the **Appendix A** part, and then start to explain the experimental part from the data processing.

3.1 Data Processing

Our experiments mainly focus on the translation from Classical Chinese to Simplified Chinese characters. In the process, the Classical Chinese text is segmented using the Jiayan Classical Chinese word segmenter, while the Modern Chinese text is segmented using the Jieba segmenter and then converted to Traditional Chinese. The Classical Chinese and Modern Chinese texts are combined and trained with 12,000 BPE subword merge operations.A discussion of the vocabulary is in **Table 3** in Appendix B.1.

The data of all subsequent experiments were expanded by 3 times using bpe-drop with a drop probability of 0.1. The results of bpe-drop are shown in **Table 4** of Appendix B.2.

3.2 Evaluation Metrics

In this paper, BLEU-4 is used as the evaluation metric for the validation set. First, the bpe is removed from the translation and candidates, then the Traditional Chinese is converted to Simplified Chinese and segmented with Jieba, and finally, the BLEU score is calculated using the multi-bleu.perl script. For the test set, the official score is used.

3.3 Experimental Settings

Our experiments are based on the open-source machine translation framework fairseq. The training parameters are: each batch contains up to 8192 subwords, the update round is 60,000, the learning rate is 0.0005, the inverse square root learning rate adjustment strategy is used, the warmup step is 4000, and the Adam optimizer is used with parameters 1=0.9, 2=0.98. During decoding, beam search with a beam width of 5 is used. The models compared are as follows:

Baseline: The baseline uses the transformer base model, both the encoder and decoder are 6 layers, the embedding dimension is 512, the feed-forward layer dimension is 2048, 8-head attention is used, and dropout is 0.2.

R-drop enhancement: R-Drop minimizes the bidirectional KL divergence between the output distributions of two sub-models sampled by dropout, thereby producing more robust output.

Span pre-training: Span corruption is to reconstruct the text spans based on the masked input document. The probability of corruption is 0.15, and the average length of spans is 3.

DAE pre-training: The denoising autoencoding task proposed in BART, which improves the performance of the model by reconstructing the text from the noised text. The probability of token mask is 0.35.

Sikuroberta parameter initialization: The model used in this paper, the encoder is 12 layers, the decoder is 6 layers, the embedding dimension is 768, the feed-forward layer dimension is 3072, 12-head attention is used, and dropout is 0.1.

Among them, 1 to 5 all use the same transformer base architecture. For the pre-training tasks of 3 and 4, they are first trained for 30,000 rounds, and then the translation task is learned.

3.4 Results

We report the validation and test set BLEU for all compared methods, as shown in **Table 1**. Compared with the baseline, rdrop improves by 0.74, while the pre-training method using span or dae improves by 1.49 and 1.26, respectively. However, we use the SikuRoBERTa initialization method to increase the BLEU score by 2.1, and the final test set score is **21.75**. Moreover, if the model of the same scale is directly trained without SikuRoBERTa initialization, the training will not converge.The display of the training effect is in **Table 5** of Appendix B.3.

Model	Valid BLEU	Test BLEU
Baseline	28.31	-
+R-Drop	29.0	-
+Span	29.80	-
+DAE	29.57	-
SikuRoBERTa-init	**30.41**	**21.75**

Table 1: EvaHan2023 Ancient Chinese Translation Closed Task (All models were trained using BPE-drop to augment data by a factor of 3)

4 Conclusion

This paper describes our submission to the 2nd International Evaluation of Automatic Analysis of Ancient Chinese (EvaHan) closed track for ancient Chinese translation. Our ancient text-modern text translation model includes two parts: bpe-drop data enhancement and parameter initialization. Future work is to combine parameter initialization and pre-training tasks simultaneously.

References

Conneau, A. and Lample, G. (2019). Cross-lingual language model pretraining. *Advances in neural information processing systems*, 32.

Devlin, J., Chang, M.-W., Lee, K., and Toutanova, K. (2018). Bert: Pre-training of deep bidirectional transformers for language understanding. *arXiv preprint arXiv:1810.04805*.

Liu, D., Yang, K., Qu, Q., and Lv, J. (2019). Ancient–modern chinese translation with a new large training dataset. *ACM Transactions on Asian and Low-Resource Language Information Processing (TALLIP)*, 19(1):1–13.

Liu, Y., Gu, J., Goyal, N., Li, X., Edunov, S., Ghazvininejad, M., Lewis, M., and Zettlemoyer, L. (2020). Multilingual denoising pre-training for neural machine translation. *Transactions of the Association for Computational Linguistics*, 8:726–742.

Pan, X., Wang, M., Wu, L., and Li, L. (2021). Contrastive learning for many-to-many multilingual neural machine translation. *arXiv preprint arXiv:2105.09501*.

Song, K., Tan, X., Qin, T., Lu, J., and Liu, T.-Y. (2019). Mass: Masked sequence to sequence pre-training for language generation. *arXiv preprint arXiv:1905.02450*.

Zhu, J., Xia, Y., Wu, L., He, D., Qin, T., Zhou, W., Li, H., and Liu, T.-Y. (2020). Incorporating bert into neural machine translation. *arXiv preprint arXiv:2002.06823*.

Appendix

A Dataset

The training datasets are respectively the parallel corpora of ancient Chinese to modern Chinese from the Twenty-Four Histories of China, the pre-Qin classics, and the "Zizhi Tongjian". The statistical data is as follows in Table X:

Data	Total volume of ancient texts	Total translations
Parallel Corpus of Twenty-Four Histories of Ancient Bai	9,583,749 Character	12,763,534 Character
Pre-Qin classics and ancient English parallel corpus of "Zi Zhi Tong Jian"	618,083 Character	838,321 Words

Table 2: EvaHan2023 training data details

Among them, the parallel corpus of ancient and modern Chinese in the Twenty-Four Histories has 307,494 lines, and the pre-Qin and "Zizhi Tongjian" have 5,899 lines. 250 pairs, a total of 500, are taken from the two corpora as the validation set.

B Some More Extra Material

B.1 Vocabulary Experiment

In order to explore the impact of word segmentation tools on model performance in ancient text translation, we used jieba and jiayan to conduct three sets of experiments. Table x shows that using jiayan and jieba word segmentation works best for ancient texts and modern texts, respectively.

No	Method	Bleu
1	Jieba_Jiaba	27.08
2	Jieba_Jiaba	27.17
3	Jiayan_Jieba	**27.89**

Table 3: Vocabulary Experiment Details

B.2 Bpe Drop

bpe drop is a data processing method that can increase data granularity and generate multivariate data, specifically as shown below.

No.	Augmented text
1	三@@ 者 同@@ 时 发生 而 又 出现 黄河 的 水@@ 清 。
2	三@@ 者 同时 发@@ 生 而 又 出现 黄河 的 水@@ 清 。
3	三@@ 者 同时 发生 而 又 出现 黄河 的 水@@ 清 。

Table 4: An example of BPE-Dropout result(Factor=3, Drop=0.1).

B.3 Model training effect

The following is the training effect of AnchiLm on the test data Id 1 and Id 100:

ID	Language	Sentence
1	An-CH	契丹侵澶，公相真宗北伐，騙河未渡。
	Mo-CH	契丹 侵犯 澶 州 ， 萊 公相 真宗 北伐 ， 臨近 黃河 沒有 渡過 黃河 。
98	An-CH	所著《索蘊》，乃其學也。
	Mo-CH	所著 的 《 索蘊 》 ， 就是 他 的 學問 。

Table 5: Case Study.

Translating Ancient Chinese to Modern Chinese at Scale: A Large Language Model-based Approach

Jiahuan Cao jiahuanc@foxmail.com
Dezhi Peng pengdzscut@foxmail.com
Yongxin Shi yongxin_shi@foxmail.com
Zongyuan Jiang eejiangzongyuan@mail.scut.edu.cn
Lianwen Jin eelwjin@scut.edu.cn
School of Electronic and Information Engineering, South China University of Technology, Guangzhou, 510641, China

Abstract

Recently, the emergence of large language models (LLMs) has provided powerful foundation models for a wide range of natural language processing (NLP) tasks. However, the vast majority of the pre-training corpus for most existing LLMs is in English, resulting in their Chinese proficiency falling far behind that of English. Furthermore, ancient Chinese has a much larger vocabulary and less available corpus than modern Chinese, which significantly challenges the generalization capacity of existing LLMs. In this paper, we investigate the Ancient-Chinese-to-Modern-Chinese (A2M) translation using LLMs including LLaMA and Ziya. Specifically, to improve the understanding of Chinese texts, we explore the vocabulary extension and incremental pre-training methods based on existing pre-trained LLMs. Subsequently, a large-scale A2M translation dataset with 4M pairs is utilized to fine-tune the LLMs. Experimental results demonstrate the effectiveness of the proposed method, especially with Ziya-13B, in translating ancient Chinese to modern Chinese. Moreover, we deeply analyze the performance of various LLMs with different strategies, which we believe can benefit further research on LLM-based A2M approaches.

1 Introduction

Ancient Chinese plays a crucial role in carrying the invaluable heritage of traditional Chinese culture. However, ancient Chinese expresses in a significantly

Proceedings of ALT2023: First Workshop on Ancient Language Translation, pages 61–69
September 5, 2023, Macau SAR, China.

different way compared with modern Chinese, which hinders the understanding of ancient Chinese books by non-experts. Therefore, automatic Ancient-Chinese-to-Modern-Chinese (A2M) translation is essential to the preservation of traditional Chinese culture.

Existing neural machine translation methods mainly adopted a sequence-to-sequence paradigm, evolving from architectures based on recurrent neural networks [1, 2], to convolutional neural networks [3], and to Transformer [4]. Although great industrial and academic success has been achieved in the neural machine translation area, the A2M translation [5, 6, 7] is still quite under-explored. With the emergence of large language models (LLMs) [8, 9], they have rapidly been applied to a wide variety of natural language processing (NLP) tasks, exhibiting high generalization and reasoning capacities. Although there have been studies [10] that attempt to use LLMs for ancient Chinese, their model sizes are limited.

To this end, we propose to solve the A2M translation problem using LLMs with large-scale parameters and datasets. Specifically, the model architecture is based on LLaMA [8] and its variants (*e.g.,* Ziya [11]). Furthermore, owing to the lack of Chinese texts in the pre-training corpus of LLaMA, we align the Chinese understanding ability of LLaMA with English using vocabulary extension and incremental pre-training following recent works [12, 13, 14]. After that, a large-scale A2M translation dataset with 4M pairs is employed to fine-tune the LLM, so as to transfer its general capacity to the specific A2M translation task. The experimental results demonstrate the effectiveness of our method, exhibiting 29.68% BLEU-4 on the testing set of the EvaHan2023 competition dataset [15].

2 Methodology

In this section, we present our approach for transferring the knowledge of a pre-trained LLM (*e.g.*, LLaMA [8]) using English pre-training corpus to the task of translating ancient Chinese to modern Chinese. As depicted in Figure 1, our approach involves three main steps, *i.e.*, vocabulary extension, incremental pre-training, and large-scale finetuning. In the following sections, we will give detailed descriptions of these steps.

2.1 Vocabulary Extension

As the original vocabulary of LLaMA lacks sufficient Chinese characters, the encoding of a single Chinese character commonly requires multiple tokens, resulting in low efficiency and unsatisfactory performance. Therefore, based on the training

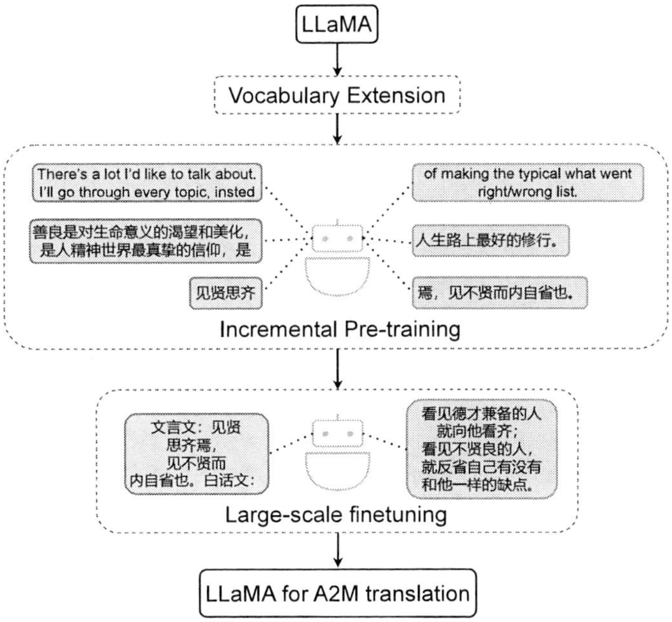

Figure 1. Overview of our method.

data of EvaHan2023, we extend 9,180 common characters and words of ancient and modern Chinese in addition to the original LLaMA vocabulary.

Furthermore, to fully utilize the knowledge of the pre-trained LLaMA, we propose DecompInit which initializes the embedding of the extended characters and words by token decomposition. As shown in Fig. 2, instead of using the popular random initialization, we initialize the embedding of a new character/word by averaging the embeddings of the tokens that it can be decomposed into. Specifically, we first denote the original LLaMA vocabulary and corresponding embeddings as $\{w_i\}_{i=1}^m$ and $\{E_i\}_{i=1}^m$, respectively, where m is the vocabulary size. Then the embedding E_{m+1} of a new word w_{m+1} that can be decomposed to $\{w_{a_i} | 1 \leq a_i \leq m\}_{i=1}^n$ is initialized as

$$E_{m+1} = \frac{1}{n} \sum_{i=1}^{n} E_{a_i}. \tag{1}$$

Empirical experiments demonstrate that this novel initialization strategy can help the model converge faster in the early stages. Moreover, the proposed DecompInit can better preserve the capacity of pre-trained LLaMA. As shown in Tab. 1, the DecompInit enables the LLaMA with extended vocabulary to generate a reasonable response to the input "你好" while the random initialization results in meaningless

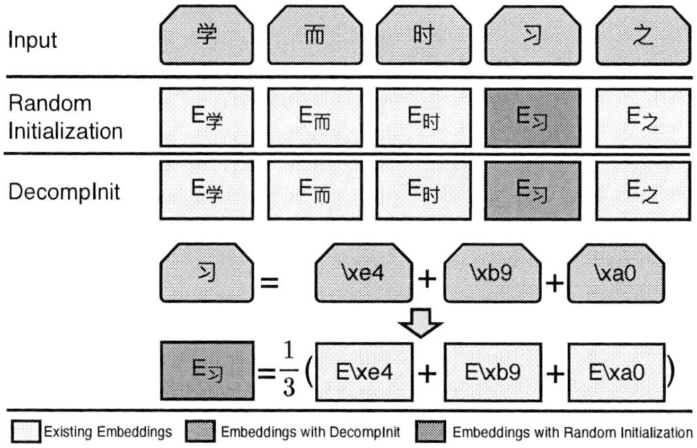

Figure 2. Illustration of the proposed DecompInit for embedding initialization.

Method	Response
Random Initialization	你 好 踐 踐\ue4bd逻 F 逻 逻 逻\n\ue4bd佾 佾 逻\n\ue4bd佾佾\n疋\n\n\n
DecompInit (Ours)	你好，我是杨晓莉，欢迎来到我的博客。\n我是一个杭州大学的学生，我的专业是计算机科学。\n我的博客是一个带有许多资料的博客，我希望能够给大家带来很多的资料。

Table 1. Comparison of model responses with random initialization and DecompInit.

outputs.

2.2 Incremental Pre-training

To further enhance the Chinese understanding capability, we conduct incremental pre-training based on LLaMA with extended vocabulary. Existing approaches to incremental pre-training are based on Chinese-only corpora [14] or mixed Chinese and English corpora [16, 11]. In this study, we validate the effectiveness of these two types of corpora. Specifically, for the Chinese-only corpora, we use Dazhige[1] and Wudao [17] for ancient Chinese and modern Chinese, respectively, while for the mixed Chinese and English corpora, we additionally incorporate Com-

[1]https://github.com/garychowcmu/daizhigev20

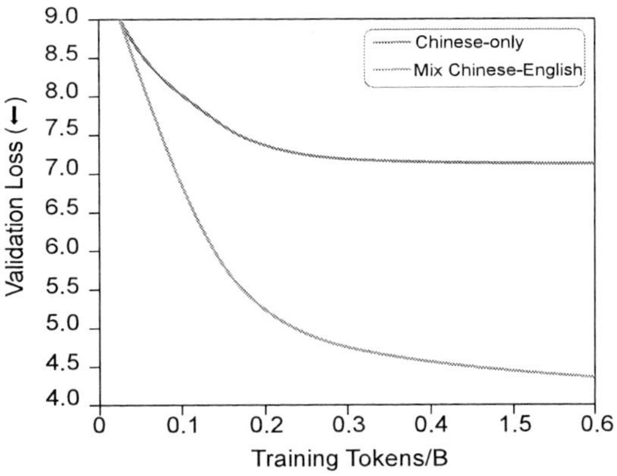

Figure 3. Validation loss on ancient Chinese.

monCrawl[2] for English. The validation loss curves on ancient Chinese of different corpora are shown in Fig. 3, which demonstrate that incorporating a mixture of Chinese and English corpora during incremental pre-training can accelerate convergence compared with using Chinese-only corpora.

2.3 Large-scale Finetuning

In order to enhance the capability of our language model in translating Ancient Chinese to Modern Chinese, we conduct large-scale finetuning using three base models, including LLaMA-7B with extended vocabulary (LLaMA-7B-EXT), LLaMA-7B with extended vocabulary and incremental pre-training (LLaMA-7B-EXT-INC), and Ziya-13B [11] that is a variant of LLaMA-13B with vocabulary extension and 110B-token incremental pre-training.

Finetuning Data. EvaHan2023 [15] originally provides 307,494 A2M translation pairs for training. We randomly sample 10,000 pairs for validation while the remaining 297,494 pairs are used for training. Moreover, we additionally use 972,467 A2M translation pairs provided by NiuTrans[3] and 2,800,000 in-house A2M translation pairs, finally yielding a large-scale finetuning dataset with 4,056,223 pairs in total.

Translation Prompts. Previous studies [18] have shown that a well-designed prompt can fully unleash the potential of large models. In our experiments, the prompt for A2M translation is "文言文：[文言文] 白话文：[白话文]", where "[文言

[2] `https://commoncrawl.org`

[3] `https://github.com/NiuTrans/Classical-Modern`

文]" represents the ancient Chinese text to translate and "[白话文]" indicates the corresponding translation in modern Chinese.

Optimization During training, the models are optimized to minimize the cross entropy loss for the tokens corresponding to the "[白话文]" part without considering the tokens of other parts, which ensures the model is focused on the translated modern Chinese text.

Inference During inference, we fill the ancient Chinese text that requires to be translated in the "[文言文]" position, yielding a translation prompt formatted as "文言文：[文言文] 白话文：". Based on this prompt, the model predicts the "[白话文]" part which is the translation result in modern Chinese.

3 Experiments

3.1 Setting

The 7B-sized models (*i.e.*, Vanilla LLaMA-7B, LLaMA-7b-EXT, and LLaMA-7B-EXT-INC) are fine-tuned with a learning rate of 2e-5, while the 13B-sized model (*i.e.*, Ziya-13B) is fine-tuned with a learning rate of 1e-5. Other experimental settings follow Vicuna[4]. We utilize the BLEU-4 [19] and CHRF-2 [20] metrics to evaluate the performance. All experiments are conducted using 8 A100 GPUs with 80GB memory.

3.2 Ablation Study on Base Model

The ablation experiments on different base models are conducted using the 297,494 training pairs from EvaHan2023. The performances on the validation set are presented in Table 2. It can be seen that the vocabulary extension and incremental pre-training contribute to significant improvement in terms of BLEU-4 and CHRF-2. Furthermore, the Ziya-13B with much more parameters than the other three base models achieves the best A2M translation performance.

3.3 Final Results

Based on the ablation results in Section 3.2, we choose Ziya-13B as the final base model. To produce the final results of the Evahan2023 competition, we fine-tune the Ziya-13B using all available data comprising 4,056,223 pairs (Section 2.3) for 5 epochs to obtain the Ziya-13B-FT1 model, and then further fine-tune the Ziya-13B-FT1 using the total EvaHan2023 competition data with 307,494 pairs for 1 epoch to obtain the Ziya-13B-FT2 model. After performing inference on the

[4]https://github.com/lm-sys/FastChat

Method	BLEU-4	CHRF-2
Vanilla LLaMA-7B [8]	59.66	56.38
LLaMA-7B-EXT	60.15	56.85
LLaMA-7B-EXT-INC	<u>60.60</u>	<u>57.49</u>
Ziya-13B [11]	**61.41**	**58.22**

Table 2. Ablation study on different base models. The performances on the validation set are reported. The bold and underline indicate the best and the second best, respectively.

test set of the Evahan2023 competition using the Ziya-13B-FT1 and Ziya-13B-FT2 models, we get two sets of final results as shown in Table 3.

Method	BLEU-4
Ziya-13B-FT1	29.54
Ziya-13B-FT2	**29.68**

Table 3. Final results on the test set of the Evahan2023 competition.

4 Conclusion

In this paper, we propose a novel approach to address the Ancient-Chinese-to-Modern-Chinese (A2M) translation task using large language models (LLMs). Specifically, based on existing pre-trained LLMs, the proposed method involves vocabulary extension, incremental pre-training, and large-scale finetuning. The experimental results demonstrate the effectiveness of our method on the A2M translation task. Moreover, the ablation study highlights the importance of vocabulary extension and incremental pre-training for LLMs to improve their understanding of low-resource languages. We believe that our findings can benefit further research on LLM-based A2M approaches and contribute to the preservation of traditional Chinese culture.

Acknowledgement

This search is supported in part by NSFC (Grant No.: 61936003).

References

[1] Ilya Sutskever, Oriol Vinyals, and Quoc V Le. Sequence to sequence learning with neural networks. In *Neural Information Processing Systems*, pages 1–9, 2014.

[2] Dzmitry Bahdanau, Kyung Hyun Cho, and Yoshua Bengio. Neural machine translation by jointly learning to align and translate. In *International Conference on Learning Representations*, pages 1–15, 2015.

[3] Jonas Gehring, Michael Auli, David Grangier, Denis Yarats, and Yann N Dauphin. Convolutional sequence to sequence learning. In *International Conference on Machine Learning*, pages 1243–1252, 2017.

[4] Ashish Vaswani, Noam Shazeer, Niki Parmar, Jakob Uszkoreit, Llion Jones, Aidan N Gomez, Łukasz Kaiser, and Illia Polosukhin. Attention is all you need. In *Neural Information Processing Systems*, pages 1–11, 2017.

[5] Dayiheng Liu, Kexin Yang, Qian Qu, and Jiancheng Lv. Ancient–modern Chinese translation with a new large training dataset. *ACM Transactions on Asian and Low-Resource Language Information Processing*, 19(1):1–13, 2019.

[6] Hongyang Zhang, Muyun Yang, and Tiejun Zhao. Exploring hybrid character-words representational unit in classical-to-modern Chinese machine translation. In *International Conference on Asian Language Processing*, pages 33–36, 2015.

[7] Zhiyuan Zhang, Wei Li, and Qi Su. Automatic translating between ancient Chinese and contemporary Chinese with limited aligned corpora. In *CCF International Conference on Natural Language Processing and Chinese Computing*, pages 157–167, 2019.

[8] Hugo Touvron, Thibaut Lavril, Gautier Izacard, Xavier Martinet, Marie-Anne Lachaux, Timothée Lacroix, Baptiste Rozière, Naman Goyal, Eric Hambro, Faisal Azhar, et al. LLaMA: Open and efficient foundation language models. *arXiv preprint arXiv:2302.13971*, 2023.

[9] OpenAI. GPT-4 technical report. *arXiv preprint arXiv:2303.08774*, 2023.

[10] Liu Chang, Wang Dongbo, Zhao Zhixiao, Hu Die, Wu Mengcheng, Lin Litao, Shen Si, Li Bin, Liu Jiangfeng, Zhang Hai, et al. SikuGPT: A generative pre-trained model for intelligent information processing of ancient texts from the perspective of digital humanities. *arXiv preprint arXiv:2304.07778*, 2023.

[11] Jiaxing Zhang, Ruyi Gan, Junjie Wang, Yuxiang Zhang, Lin Zhang, Ping Yang, Xinyu Gao, Ziwei Wu, Xiaoqun Dong, Junqing He, Jianheng Zhuo, Qi Yang, Yongfeng Huang, Xiayu Li, Yanghan Wu, Junyu Lu, Xinyu Zhu, Weifeng Chen, Ting Han, Kunhao Pan, Rui Wang, Hao Wang, Xiaojun Wu, Zhongshen Zeng, and Chongpei Chen. Fengshenbang 1.0: Being the foundation of Chinese cognitive intelligence. *arXiv preprint arXiv:2209.02970*, 2022.

[12] Yunjie Ji, Yan Gong, Yong Deng, Yiping Peng, Qiang Niu, Baochang Ma, and Xiangang Li. Towards better instruction following language models for Chinese: Investigating the impact of training data and evaluation. *arXiv preprint arXiv:2304.07854*, 2023.

[13] Haochun Wang, Chi Liu, Nuwa Xi, Zewen Qiang, Sendong Zhao, Bing Qin, and Ting Liu. Huatuo: Tuning LLaMA model with Chinese medical knowledge. *arXiv preprint arXiv:2304.06975*, 2023.

[14] Yiming Cui, Ziqing Yang, and Xin Yao. Efficient and effective text encoding for Chinese LLaMA and Alpaca. *arXiv preprint arXiv:2304.08177*, 2023.

[15] Dongbo Wang, Si Shen, Minxuan Feng, Chao Xu, Lianzhen Zhao, Wenlong Sun, Bin Li, Liu Liu, and Wenhao Ye. Evahan2023. `https://github.com/GoThereGit/EvaHan`, 2023.

[16] Zhongli Li. Billa: A bilingual LLaMA with enhanced reasoning ability. `https://github.com/Neutralzz/BiLLa`, 2023.

[17] Sha Yuan, Hanyu Zhao, Zhengxiao Du, Ming Ding, Xiao Liu, Yukuo Cen, Xu Zou, Zhilin Yang, and Jie Tang. WuDaoCorpora: A super large-scale Chinese corpora for pre-training language models. *AI Open*, 2:65–68, 2021.

[18] Daniel Khashabi, Shane Lyu, Sewon Min, Lianhui Qin, Kyle Richardson, Sean Welleck, Hannaneh Hajishirzi, Tushar Khot, Ashish Sabharwal, Sameer Singh, et al. Prompt waywardness: The curious case of discretized interpretation of continuous prompts. *arXiv preprint arXiv:2112.08348*, 2021.

[19] Kishore Papineni, Salim Roukos, Todd Ward, and Wei-Jing Zhu. BLEU: A method for automatic evaluation of machine translation. In *Association for Computational Linguistics*, pages 311–318, 2002.

[20] Maja Popović. CHRF: Character n-gram F-score for automatic MT evaluation. In *Workshop on Statistical Machine Translation*, pages 392–395, 2015.

Author Index